THE
TRUSTING
HEART

THE TRUSTING HEART

GREAT NEWS
ABOUT
TYPE A BEHAVIOR

Redford Williams, M.D.

Times BOOKS

For Virginia

Grateful acknowledgment is made to the Division of Christian Education of
the National Council of the Churches of Christ in the USA for permission to
reprint Bible text from the Revised Standard Version Bible. Copyright 1946,
1952, © 1971 by the Division of Christian Education of the National Council
of the Churches of Christ in the USA. Used by permission.

Designed by Oksana Kushnir

Library of Congress Cataloging-in-Publication Data

Williams, Redford Brown.
The trusting heart.

Bibliography: p.
Includes index.
1. Coronary heart disease—Psychosomatic aspects.
2. Coronary heart disease—Prevention.   3. Type A
behavior.   I. Title.
RC685.C6W55   1989   616.1'208   88-40168
ISBN 0-8129-1675-1

Manufactured in the United States of America
9 8 7 6 5 4 3 2
First Edition

PREFACE

As an academician accustomed to writing for a scientific audience, I undertook with some trepidation the writing of a book for a general audience. Translating complex scientific concepts and research findings into language that the nonprofessional reader can understand requires a willingness often to sacrifice some of the scientist's cherished precision of exposition for the sake of conceptual clarity and intelligibility.

I felt it important to make the effort, however, in order to clarify the confusion that has come to cloud the public's understanding of Type A behavior and its relationship to heart disease. I believe much of this confusion can be dispelled by recent research findings, some of which I've contributed to, on coronary-prone behavior, and I wanted to spread the good news. I was encouraged that I might be able to do this effectively by the warm reception I have received when speaking on this topic to a variety of non-professional groups, including both healthy individuals and patients with heart disease.

There are many people whose aid over the years has been important in helping me arrive at the point where I could contemplate writing this book. Still, any deficiencies are my responsibility. In naming those to whom I am indebted, I will undoubtedly omit some who should be named. I ask their pardon for my oversights.

As a freshman at Harvard, I took a seminar in the behavioral sciences with Dr. George W. Goethals III. Our first assignment was to write a paper on "the mind-body problem." George's enthusiastic approach to teaching us about behavioral science inspired me to continue learning in this field, and his wisdom guided me toward a productive path. In a very real sense, this book is the continuation of that freshman assignment. Also at Harvard, Dr. Stanley H. King provided me with a model of the behavioral scientist hard at work to apply knowledge to the solution of important human problems.

In medical school at Yale, Dr. F. Patrick McKegney took me under his wing and taught me the research craft. The expectation at Yale that every medical student would write a thesis based on his or her own research, and the funds that were provided to support us in this pursuit, played an important part in my evolution into a researcher. Other Yale mentors included Drs. Phillip Bondy, Thomas Detre, Al Feinstein, Chase Kimball, Patrick Mulrow, and Morton Reiser.

After Yale I spent two years as a clinical associate at the National Institute of Mental Health, where my horizons were expanded by mentors like Drs. Monte Buchsbaum, Philipe Cardon, Irwin Kopin, Frederick Snyder, Lyman Wynne, and Ted Zahn; and by such like-aged peers as Drs. Burr Eichelman, Bernard Frankel, Christian Gillin,

Friedhelm Lamprecht, Gus Watanabe, James Weiss, Fred Wooten, and Richard Wyatt.

Since joining the faculty at Duke in 1972, I have been fortunate to benefit from interactions with several colleagues, including Drs. John Barefoot, Jorge Bartolome, Marianne Breslin, Rob Califf, Doyle Gentry, Thom Haney, Frank Harrell, Mark Hlatky, Frank Keefe, Dave Kong, Cindy Kuhn, Kerry Lee, Gail Marsh, Jim Morris, Charles Nemeroff, David Pryor, Ilene Siegler, Maddie Spach, Gene Stead, Richard Surwit, Larry Thompson, Jay Weiss, Bob Whalen, Sandy Williams, and many others. A special acknowledgment goes to Dr. Saul Schanberg, who has been mentor, colleague, and friend at every step along the way. I have also had the good luck to have supportive and caring chairmen in the Department of Psychiatry: Drs. Ewald Busse, Keith Brodie, and Bernard Carroll.

It has been said that the real reason for having students is not only to teach them but also to learn from them. This has certainly been true for me. Among those trainees I have been fortunate to learn from through the years are Drs. Norman Anderson, Guillermo Bernal, Jim Blumenthal, Shin Fukudo, Alberto Grignolo, Jim Lane, Paul Mohl, Hirokazu Monou, Motoyazu Muranaka, Leonard Poon, Edward Suarez, and Fumihito Taguchi.

Outside of Duke, there are many colleagues whose help along the way has made important contributions to much of what I have accomplished. First of all, Drs. Ray Rosenman and Meyer Friedman have always been willing to share their knowledge and insights about coronary-prone behavior, not only with me but also with a host of others. Without their guidance and encouragement in the early stages, I would not be able now to write this book.

Among other behavioral medicine colleagues to whom much credit must go for helping me in innumerable ways are Drs. Herbert Benson, Joseph Brady, Margaret Chesney, Thomas Clarkson, Paul Costa, Grant Dahlstrom, Ted

Dembroski, Joel Dimsdale, Robert Eliot, Bernard Engel, Marianne Frankenhaeuser, Mats Frederickson, David Glass, Jim Henry, Alan Herd, Shigeaki Hinohara, David Jenkins, Stevo Julius, Bert Kaplan, Jay Kaplan, Donald Kornfeld, David Krantz, John and Beatrice Lacey, Stephen Manuck, Karen Matthews, Neal Miller, Paul Obrist, Judith Rodin, Richard Rose, Neil Schneiderman, Gary Schwartz, David Shapiro, Charles Spielberger, and Jinichi Suzuki, to name but a few.

My research has been generously supported by the federal government. The Research Scientist Development Program of the National Institute of Mental Health has provided salary support since 1974. Without the freedom to pursue my research that came with this support, it is doubtful I would have been able to persevere. The National Heart, Lung, and Blood Institute has provided generous support for my research program since 1976. Special recognition goes to Drs. Steve Weiss and Jim Shields for encouraging and sticking with many of us interested in behavioral medicine through the occasionally traumatic NIH peer review process. Other important research support has come from the John D. and Catherine T. MacArthur Foundation, the Upjohn Company, and Ayerst Laboratories.

Without help, guidance, and encouragement from those I have named above, the science described in this book would not have been possible. Without the excellent editoral help from my editors Jonathan Segal and Sarah Trotta, my copy editor, and others at Times Books, I would not have been able to tell you about this research nearly as well as I have. To the extent I fall short, the responsibility is totally my own.

Without the able administrative assistance of Linda Jackson in all aspects of my work here at Duke, I would not have been able to find the time to write this book, not to mention doing many other worthwhile things. Thanks also

to Muriel Roll for her excellent help in all phases of putting
this book on paper.

On a more personal note, I want to acknowledge the
role my family has played in whatever success I have
gained in my work. My father, Redford Williams, Sr., who
died last September after a six-month battle with cancer,
taught me the importance of sticking with whatever jobs
you take on. Equally important, he made sure I learned
how to do this. My mother's courage during his last months
was a source of inspiration for me. My children, Jennifer
and Lloyd, have always been a source of great support.
Such loving, enthusiastic offspring make it hard for anyone
to remain a hostile heart.

Finally, I will never be able to find words adequate
enough to describe how important in all aspects of my life
has been the love, support, companionship, and intellectual
sharing that has been my blessing in having a wife like
Virginia. Much of what is good in this book is due to her
help at all steps along the way. More than anyone else, she
has helped me to have a more trusting heart.

June 1988
Durham, N.C.

INTRODUCTION

America is a health-conscious nation. Each year we spend billions of dollars on products and services with the hope of reducing our risk of developing life-threatening illnesses, curing or ameliorating maladies we already have, and improving our emotional and physical health.

Stimulated by massive public health advertising efforts, millions of Americans have stopped smoking, cut fatty foods out of their diets, had their blood pressure checked, and taken up jogging. And it appears that these changes in our behavior have paid off, at least for some health problems. Since the early 1970s, deaths due to our major killer, coronary heart disease, have shown a steady decline. Medical experts believe that at least some of this fall in coronary death rates is the result of the better health practices taken up by the American public.

The picture is not entirely rosy, however, and there

continues to be much room for further improvement. Cancer deaths, for example, continue to climb, despite real progress in treating some forms of this dread disease. And, though deaths due to heart disease have fallen, coronary heart disease continues to be the number-one killer in the United States, accounting for more than twice as many deaths as all forms of cancer each year.

Clearly, then, there must be additional steps we can take to improve our health and reduce our chances of suffering serious illnesses. Many medical experts believe that such progress is next likely to involve the development of effective means to cut the toll exacted by psychological stress.

The strongest case for targeting stress's role in human illness can be found in the voluminous research concerning the relationship between Type A behavior and coronary heart disease. As a result of pioneering research by two San Francisco cardiologists, Meyer Friedman and Ray Rosenman, nearly every American is now aware that Type As are people who are always in a hurry, keenly ambitious and competitive, and easily moved to hostility and anger by everyday annoyances. Nearly everyone also has known, until recently at least, that Type As are at much higher risk of suffering a heart attack or dying from coronary disease than their less impatient, less competitive, and less hostile Type B counterparts.

Just as the American public was about ready to add Type A behavior to the list of those risk factors—smoking, high cholesterol levels, high blood pressure, and too little physical exercise—needing attention in their self-improvement programs, reports began to appear suggesting that perhaps the Type A story was not as simple as it had first seemed. Many studies, for example, failed to find increased risk of heart attacks in Type As.

The confusion occasioned by these negative studies, which began to appear in the late 1970s, is now starting to clear—the result of major research efforts at various centers around the U.S. aimed at clarifying and refining our understanding of the relationship between Type A behavior and coronary heart disease.

As an active participant in this "second generation" research on Type A behavior, I recently concluded that the time is ripe to tell the American public what this research has found.

I believe the research findings are now sufficiently clear that we can be confident in telling you the good news and the bad news about Type A behavior. The good news is this: Not all aspects of Type A behavior are equally toxic. It now seems clear that being in a hurry and being ambitious and competitive are not, *taken alone*, putting you at risk of having a heart attack or dying from coronary disease.

Now for the bad news: Hostility, anger, and their biological consequences are the toxic part of Type A behavior. Hostility and anger not only account for the increased risk of developing coronary heart disease among Type A persons, but may also increase the risk of suffering other life-threatening illnesses as well. The other aspects of Type A behavior—e.g., being in a hurry and being competitive—appear to be harmful only to the extent that they activate one's hostility and anger.

It follows, therefore, that the most important thing you can do to decrease your coronary risk if you are a Type A person is to learn to reduce your hostility and anger. If yours is a hostile heart, you need to change it into a more trusting heart; the new research described in this book shows that it is the trusting heart that enjoys a longer and healthier life.

My purpose, then, is twofold: First, to convince you that hostility and anger are indeed harmful to your health and well-being. To accomplish this, part 1 of this book will describe the research findings responsible for my present confidence regarding the good and bad news about Type A.

The second purpose, and the focus of part 2, is to provide you with a practical guide that will enable you (a) to recognize your own hostility and anger and (b) to take the steps necessary to reduce these toxic influences in your relationships with the people you deal with every day.

What can you expect to gain from this book? If you absorb the knowledge presented in part 1 and build upon it by putting into practice the steps described in part 2, I believe you can count on two potentially beneficial outcomes.

First, you will almost certainly find your interpersonal relationships with other people—strangers, friends, family, even "enemies"—a source of greater pleasure and satisfaction than before. In other words, you will be a more pleasant person to be around, and this may lead you to find others more pleasant to be around, too.

Second, you will probably improve your health (there are never any guarantees) as a result of eliminating those personal characteristics shown by new research to increase risk of disease and death. By learning to trust others more, you will be taking the steps necessary to eliminate hostility and anger from your daily life, thereby blunting their harmful biological effects on your body.

CONTENTS

PART ONE

THE GOOD AND BAD NEWS ABOUT TYPE A BEHAVIOR

ONE

"...BUT WORDS CAN ALSO HURT ME"

I t had been a quiet morning in the Boston suburb that was home to the woman we will call Mary Smith. Except for being slightly overweight, at 44 she was in reasonably good health. Our knowledge of her personal life is sketchy; we have no information regarding her relationships with family or friends, her work situation, or even the makeup of her family.

We do know that she had a 17-year-old son, and that sometime during the afternoon following this particular morning she received word that he had committed suicide. Her reaction to this catastrophic news was not recorded, but we can well imagine that she experienced acute emotional distress of an intensity not felt by most of us in a lifetime.

It is recorded that half an hour after learning of her son's death she developed "severe 'crushing' substernal pain . . . with radiation to the left shoulder." This pain in the middle of her chest not only continued but worsened, and after six hours she was taken to a local hospital, where her medical saga began to unfold.

Not surprisingly, the doctors at the hospital suspected a heart attack was in progress and obtained an electrocardiogram. It was completely normal. The pain in Mary Smith's chest was getting worse, however, so they gave her nitroglycerin tablets under her tongue, hoping this treatment would relax the arteries supplying blood to the heart. No relief.

The plot thickened. Since her blood pressure fell to dangerously low levels, an intravenous saline drip was started. Her blood pressure rose to a safe level, but she began to have "ventricular ectopic beats," which could lead to a life-threatening disturbance of the heart's rhythmic pumping action. The emergency-room doctors started an intravenous drip of lidocaine, a local anesthetic that is often used to quiet extra beats. Unfortunately, it also suppresses the heart's pumping action, and Mary Smith's blood pressure plummeted again. Her chest pain grew even more severe. She began to sweat profusely, a bad sign. More intravenous saline was given.

Two hours after arriving at the hospital, she had received well over two quarts of fluid by vein. Suddenly, in addition to all her other symptoms, she began to have difficulty breathing. The doctor who listened to her chest heard crackling noises with each inspiration. Instead of the normal two heart sounds, "lub—dub," there were three, "lub—duh—duh." These signs and symptoms indicated that Mary Smith had now developed the ominous condition of pulmonary edema—her failing heart could no longer pump the blood delivered to it, and the fluid was backing up into her lungs. A chest X ray confirmed the clinical impression. Another electrocardiogram was obtained, but, much to everyone's surprise, it was still normal.

Given her deteriorating condition, Mary Smith was transferred to the intensive care unit. To enable the doctors to monitor her condition more closely, a tube was inserted into the large vein in her leg and advanced through the right side of her heart out into the pulmonary artery, the large vessel that carries blood to the lungs to pick up oxygen before it is pumped by the left side of the heart to the body's tissues. As expected, the pressures in the heart's right side and the pulmonary artery were elevated, reflecting the fluid back-up. Diuretics were administered to reduce the fluid overload, thereby lessening the work required of the heart. Other drugs were given to constrict the arteries and maintain the blood pressure as well.

The next morning, Mary Smith's condition appeared to stabilize. The blood pressure was still low, but the pain in her chest stopped and her breathing came more easily. Studies of the oxygen content of her blood suggested that she did not have a blood clot in her lungs. While the enzymes that indicate heart muscle damage in patients suffering a heart attack were somewhat elevated in her blood, they were not at the high levels to be expected in someone who had had a heart attack.

Mary Smith was a difficult puzzle for her doctors at this point. She was clearly very sick, sick enough to die. Yet the obvious causes of such a clinical picture—heart attack or blood clot in the lung—were not confirmed by the studies performed thus far. She was transferred to another hospital, where even more sophisticated diagnostic and treatment resources could be brought into action.

And they were. A balloon pump was inserted into her aorta to assist her heart's pumping action. There was an almost immediate fall in the elevated pressures on her heart's right side. Next, to evaluate the vessels supplying blood to her heart's muscle, a tube was inserted into her coronary arteries and dye was injected. The X-ray pictures of Mary Smith's coronary arteries surprised everyone connected with her case. Contrary to expectation, there were no severe arteriosclerotic blockages of the sort that would explain why she was so sick. There was no indication of a coronary thrombosis, or blood clot, the usual precipitating event in a heart attack.

The X-ray study did reveal some serious abnormalities, however. In patchy areas scattered throughout the left ventricle, the muscular pump that sends oxygenated blood throughout the body, the muscle was either not contracting or was contracting only weakly, and this poor function could well be responsible for her catastrophic illness.

But why was the heart muscle so impaired in doing its work? A heart attack could cause such impairment, but all the test results were strongly against the diagnosis of myocardial infarction. To answer the question as to cause, another tube was passed, this time via an artery, into the left ventricle of Mary Smith's heart. This tube contained a tiny "grabber" whose jaws could snip off little pieces of the poorly contracting heart muscle, which were then sucked out through the tube and sent to the pathology department for detailed examination using several methods, including the most up-to-date, sophisticated techniques of molecular biology.

Examination of the tissue fragments using the ordinary light microscope showed multiple small patches containing dead or dying heart muscle cells, often in conjunction with white blood cells of the sort seen surrounding an inflammation. Special stains indicated that nonspecific antibodies had accumulated around the damaged heart cells as well, strengthening the growing suspicion that some sort of inflammatory response had occurred.

A special "antimyosin-antibody cardiac imaging" study was performed next. Antibodies to another antibody, in this case to myosin, the major molecule in heart muscle cells, were labeled with a radioactive isotope and injected into one of Mary Smith's veins. Pictures taken with a nuclear camera revealed antibody accumulation in the same areas of Mary Smith's heart that had not been contracting in the earlier X-ray study. In all likelihood, the antibody to the myosin molecule was concentrated in these areas because the heart cells there had been damaged, this damage had exposed the myosin within the cells to the immune system, and the antibodies to the myosin were formed and attached to the damaged cells, where they were detected by the antibody to the antimyosin antibody.

Following this final diagnostic procedure, Mary Smith was treated with drugs to suppress her immune system. She improved rapidly, and by the time all medications were stopped six months later, she was essentially back to her normal physical condition.

So far, all well and good. An apparently healthy 44-year-old woman nearly died of a sudden insult to her heart—an insult that was so severe that it caused the death of many heart cells, enough, in fact, to cause the heart nearly to fail in its life-sustaining function as a pump. All of this was discovered using the most modern and sophisticated facilities of one of the world's foremost medical centers. But one key piece of the puzzle was still missing: Just exactly what was it that damaged those heart cells in the first place?

The final diagnosis reported by the pathologists was "myocarditis, acute, idiopathic," which is simply to say inflammation of the heart, sudden onset, and we don't know what caused it. They were willing to speculate on possible causes, however:

> Although the cause of the myocarditis is unknown, in most cases of myocarditis it is believed to be of viral origin. We cannot exclude, however, the possibility that this patient had a stress induced myocarditis caused by

high circulating levels of catecholamines [e.g., adrena-
line] producing isolated myocyte necrosis [heart cell
death], either by causing vasospasm or directly by damaging the cells.

The case of the woman I have called Mary Smith was
first published in the May 8, 1986, issue of *The New England Journal of Medicine*. I have chosen to begin this book
with her case because it is one of the latest, as well as one
of the most clearly documented, on record of sudden
death (or "near death," the basic mechanisms being the
same) occurring in the setting of profound emotional
arousal. That she made it to the hospital enabled doctors
to determine what happened in her case to an extent that
is not usually possible.

Along with a multitude of similar anecdotal reports
(see chapter 2), the detailed information from the case of
Mary Smith makes a strong circumstantial case for the
impact of states of mind upon the well-being of the heart
and body. But this kind of evidence alone does not constitute the sort of ultimate scientific proof that is necessary
before a skeptical medical community will begin in earnest
to devise methods to prevent or treat the effects of emotions
upon the body.

Even such well-documented cases as Mary Smith's are
no more final proof of negative mind-body interactions
than stories of miracle cures are proof of positive effects.
Such proof requires an accumulation of solid epidemiological evidence, studies of thousands of individuals, wherein
the presence of the proposed risk factor—whether a physical condition such as high blood cholesterol levels or a state
of mind such as emotional shock—is clearly shown to predict increased risk of illness. Equally essential is that laboratory studies provide convincing evidence that the
proposed risk factor actually leads, via identified biological
pathways, to disease.

This latter step solidifies the scientific case, but, more important, usually points the way to the most efficient and effective means of prevention and treatment. For example, the demonstration that a specific virus causes poliomyelitis led to the development of a vaccine that effectively abolished this disease as a public health problem.

Just such a program of rigorous epidemiological and laboratory research has been under way for two decades and has led many in both the lay and medical communities to conclude that states of mind do play an important causative role in coronary heart disease, America's number-one killer. Credit for starting this research belongs to two San Francisco cardiologists, Meyer Friedman and Ray Rosenman, whose extensive studies on the Type A behavior pattern made the most convincing case that one's personality and behavior can increase the risk of developing coronary heart disease.

Since the publication of their landmark book, *Type A Behavior and Your Heart*, "Type A" has become a part of nearly everyone's vocabulary. The term describes a person who is always in a hurry, is driven by a nearly insatiable drive for success, and is easily stirred to anger by even trivial annoyances. In their classic Western Collaborative Group Study, Friedman and Rosenman showed that Type A men were about twice as likely as those without the above characteristics, whom they termed "Type B," to develop coronary disease over an 8½-year follow-up period.

At present, over two thousand papers on various aspects of Type A behavior have been published in scientific and medical journals, not to mention many books and magazine articles intended for the lay reader. But not all of the research has confirmed the initial results of the Type A research. Following the earlier studies (which delineated increased heart attack rates and even increased arteriosclerotic blockages in the coronary arteries of Type A individuals) there have been a number of recent studies that failed to find increased coronary disease rates among Type As. In fact, a 1988 paper in *The New England Journal of Medicine* reported that, after a heart attack, Type As actually lived *longer* than Type Bs.

Thus, the early promise of the Type A research has now become clouded. While earlier, nearly everyone was ready to undergo "de-Type A-ification"—to learn to slow down, cool off, and take it easy to avoid a heart attack— there is now a great deal of confusion. Is Type A really a risk factor for coronary heart disease? Is it actually *protective* once one has had a heart attack, and are interventions to reduce Type A behavior in heart patients therefore useless, or even likely to be harmful? Are all the aspects of Type A behavior equally harmful, or are some more harmful than others? If only some aspects are harmful, how does this harm come about? And, finally, what does all this portend for how you, as a person concerned about reducing your risk of suffering a heart attack, should attempt to cope with your own Type A behavior?

Recent research does provide encouraging answers to these questions. Along with the research that has failed to confirm earlier Type A results, a systematic research program at several U.S. medical centers has been conducted during the past decade with the goal of refining the Type A hypothesis. This research aims to identify those specific aspects of Type A behavior that are and are not toxic to the heart, as well as the biological pathways whereby such effects occur.

This book is about what this new research has shown us that is useful in understanding the role played by the mind and emotions in coronary heart disease (as well as other serious diseases). This research has shown that not all aspects of Type A behavior are equally toxic. In fact, while some are clearly toxic, others appear to be not only harmless but potentially of some protective benefit. By isolating with more precision those psychological and associated biological characteristics that lead to health problems, it should be possible to identify more specific targets for our efforts to reduce coronary risk.

As we shall learn in the pages ahead, those aspects of Type A behavior concerned with hostility and anger are toxic, while those aspects concerned with rapid accomplishment of tasks and the achievement of lofty career goals are at least not toxic and may even, when not associated with hostility and anger, confer some protection. We shall learn that the benefits of having a "trusting heart," supported by the most recent modern research, have been understood and counseled by the core teachings of the world's great religions for over two millennia.

We shall learn also that the links between the trusting heart and the healthy heart are based on biological principles that can be examined using the most rigorous modern research techniques. We shall learn that there appear to be specific biological correlates of hostility and anger that can lead to disease, while specific biological correlates of trust and positive emotions can be health promoting.

Finally, and perhaps most important for you the reader, we shall learn how this new research leads to specific ways you can help yourself. Behavior modification, religion, and medicine each can provide ways of encouraging a trusting heart in yourself.

Research has already shown that if heart attack victims can learn to trust others and curb their free-floating hostility and angry reactions, their risk of suffering another heart attack is reduced. While harder to prove, it is likely that the benefits of such changes can be even greater for those who have not yet suffered heart damage: It is far easier to patch a small hole in the dike than it is to stem the flood once a breach occurs.

But we are getting ahead of our story. Let us return now to the beginning, and see how Friedman and Rosenman advanced from anecdote to epidemiology in formulating and testing the Type A hypothesis—how the bandwagon that made "Type A" a part of the American lexicon was set in motion, how it derailed, and how the correct path was eventually found.

TWO

FROM ANECDOTE
TO EPIDEMIOLOGY

As scientific pioneers reminisce, they often recall past events that, though unappreciated at the time, nevertheless had an impact on their thinking and thereby prepared the way for the eventual emergence of a new idea. Such an event occurred in the mid-1950s, when an upholsterer noticed an unusual pattern of wear on the chairs in the waiting room of Drs. Meyer Friedman and Ray Rosenman: While the fabric elsewhere was virtually like new, the *front edge* of the seats was badly frayed. The upholsterer described his observation to their office receptionist, who, in turn, mentioned it to Dr. Friedman. Although he did not feel it worth much thought at the time, Dr. Friedman later realized that this apparently trivial observation may have been the start of his and Dr. Rosenman's pioneering research to expand our understanding of the causes of coronary heart disease. But first, let's set the scene.

Since the first quarter of this century, coronary heart disease has been and continues to be the major cause of death in the U.S. and other industrialized nations, despite a recent decrease in mortality due to heart disease. More than half of all the deaths every year in the United States are attributable to diseases of the heart and blood vessels. Since many of these deaths occur in men during their most productive middle years, the social costs and psychological suffering caused by lethal and nonlethal forms of coronary disease defy comprehension. The economic impact has been estimated to exceed $100 billion per year.

Following the promulgation of the germ theory of disease in the nineteenth century, modern medicine has emphasized the search for a specific, and usually single, cause for each disease. The conquest of pneumonia by penicillin and of smallpox and polio by the development of vaccines attest to the success of this "one disease, one cause" approach. It appears likely that this approach will also be needed to deal with the growing AIDS epidemic.

In contrast to its successes in coping with infectious diseases, however, this approach has not solved the problems of the more complex, chronic diseases that now account for most of our health costs. It is now accepted that multiple factors (rather than a single causative agent) play major roles in the causation of today's primary killers, coronary disease and cancer.

At about the time Dr. Friedman's upholsterer was noticing the unusual wear pattern on the reception-room chairs, cardiologists in Framingham, Massachusetts, began to track several thousand inhabitants of that Boston suburb. Until that time, an array of circumstantial evidence (i.e., comparisons between heart attack victims and healthy persons) suggested that a number of characteristics, such as cigarette smoking, high levels of cholesterol in the blood, and high blood pressure, were more often present in those who had suffered a heart attack than in those who had not.

Since association does not prove causation, however, it was necessary to mount a large-scale prospective study to show that the presence of these characteristics, or "risk factors," actually predicted an increased risk of later developing coronary disease.

The now world-famous Framingham Study was a signal success in that regard. Within a decade, the Framingham research team was able to demonstrate to nearly everyone's satisfaction that high cholesterol, cigarette smoking, and high blood pressure were indeed very reliable predictors of increased risk of subsequent heart attacks—as well as of deaths due to coronary disease—in the Framingham population. Subsequent research has refined and improved the early results. For example, we now know that the cholesterol story is not as simple as once thought. The total amount of cholesterol that circulates in the bloodstream is a complex mixture of several forms of fat, only some of which—the low-density lipoprotein (LDL)—is toxic, while some—the high-density lipoprotein (HDL)—is actually protective of the blood vessels supplying the heart muscle.

As a result of the Framingham findings, massive public health programs are now under way that promote the adoption of diets intended to reduce blood cholesterol levels, campaign for the early identification and treatment of high blood pressure, and encourage people to stop smoking. Undoubtedly these measures are responsible, at least in part, for the reduction in coronary disease mortality over the past decade.

But the success has been far from complete. While high blood pressure detection and treatment programs have had a dramatic impact on the reduction of stroke and other problems arising in the arteries supplying the brain, these programs have had only a small impact on the risk of developing arteriosclerosis (hardening of the arteries by fatty deposits) in the blood vessels that supply the muscle of the heart. Similarly, massive efforts to reduce not only high blood pressure but high cholesterol and smoking as well, such as the $100 million Multiple Risk Factor Intervention Trial (or MRFIT) study, did not lead to the expected dramatic reductions in coronary disease.

Although Drs. Friedman and Rosenman could not have foreseen these developments in the late 1950s when they began their Type A research, they did know that the traditional risk factors did not account for most of the heart attacks and heart-related deaths that occur. That is, among those persons who develop coronary disease, at least half the heart attacks could not be explained by the presence of any known risk factors. Clearly, Friedman and Rosenman reasoned, there was a need to identify and understand new risk factors, beyond those already known, if we were to reduce the toll of coronary heart disease.

Their own extensive experience in caring for heart attack victims led them to believe that they might discover a new sort of risk factor in the psychological realm. But this clinical experience, their subsequent discovery of the Type A behavior pattern and its association with coronary heart disease, did not occur in a vacuum. Long before Friedman and Rosenman began to muse about personality and heart disease, others had noticed the impact of the mind and emotions upon the body.

HISTORICAL ANTECEDENTS
OF THE TYPE A HYPOTHESIS

The notion that states of mind can influence the functioning and the health of the body is by no means a modern idea. As far back as there is a written record, in fact, is evidence that keen observers were aware of such influences. Over forty-five hundred years ago, as we learn in surviving medical "textbooks," such as the Ebers and Edwin Smith papyri, physicians in ancient Egypt knew that in touching the limbs of a patient they were examining the heart, "because all his limbs possess its vessels, that is: the heart speaks out of the vessels of every limb." Historians of medicine interpret these ancient documents as suggesting that Egyptian physicians were aware of the influences of exercise, fear, and fever upon the heart and the pulse. Indeed, the priests of Sekhmet may have even been specialists in examining the pulse and arriving at a diagnosis based on its quality and possibly even its rate.

Perhaps the first recorded instance of sudden death occurring in the setting of emotional distress is to be found in the Bible, in the fifth chapter of the Acts of the Apostles. There it is told that Ananias and his wife, Sapphira, sold a parcel of land but dishonestly offered only part of the proceeds to Peter, keeping some of the money for themselves. Peter took Ananias to task for this, saying, " 'How is it that thou has conceived this thing in thy heart? Thou has not lied unto men, but unto God.' And Ananias hearing these words fell down and gave up the ghost." About three hours later, the scripture continues, Sapphira returned, and, not knowing what had happened, told Peter that what they had offered him was all they had received for the land they sold. Peter confronted her as he had Ananias: " 'How is it that ye have agreed together to try the Spirit of the Lord? Behold the feet of them that have buried thy husband are at the door and they shall carry thee out.' And she fell down immediately at his feet and gave up the ghost."

In *Claudius the God,* the sequel to his novel *I, Claudius,* Robert Graves describes another incident that was recorded in the Acts of the Apostles. After King Herod acknowledges the homage of the delegates from Tyre and Sidon and the adoration of the assembled masses, accepting by his very words their description of him as a god, an owl flies into the stadium and perches on a rope just above

Herod's left shoulder. This reminded Herod that in accepting godlike status he had broken the first and greatest command passed down through Moses: "Thou shalt have no other Gods but me." Within five days he was dead, with maggot-infested sores covering his body.

Just as the deaths of Ananias and Sapphira may be the first recorded instances of sudden cardiac death, it is tempting to speculate that Herod's death may be the first example of a stress-induced disease characterized by impaired immune function.

Over the centuries, two Roman emperors, a Catholic pope, and a king of Spain have been reported to have died suddenly while in the throes of acute emotional distress. One of the best documented such events was the death of the distinguished eighteenth-century English surgeon Sir John Hunter. Hunter is quoted as saying, "My life is in the hands of any rascal who chooses to annoy and tease me." He apparently had noted a link between his frequent attacks of anginal chest pain and run-ins with his colleagues. On an evening in 1793, his prediction proved accurate: After a heated argument with other doctors at a hospital board meeting, Hunter stalked out to an adjoining room, gave a deep groan, and fell dead.

In addition to these rather dramatic cases, some systematic investigation bearing on relationships between the emotions and the heart was also going on. In 1628, William Harvey, regarded as one of the founders of modern physiology and medicine, published in London a book that even today stands as an excellent example of the scientific method. In this book *De motu cordis et sanguinis* (the motion of the heart and blood), Harvey provided the first documented description of the circulation of the blood: from the left side of the heart via the arteries to the bodily tissues, back via the veins to the right side of the heart, whence via the pulmonary artery to the lungs and then back to the left side of the heart, where the cycle is renewed.

Harvey could not know that the ancient Egyptians had surmised at least part of that story more than four thousand years earlier—that the heart "spoke" to the limbs via vessels extending from it. There was another, even more striking, similarity between Harvey and his ancient predecessors. Just as with the ancient Egyptian physicians who specialized in examining the pulse, Harvey's observations led him to conclude that in addition to the heart speaking to the limbs via the arteries, the mind also speaks to the heart. As he put it in 1628, "Every affection of the mind that is attended with either pain or pleasure, hope or fear, is the cause of an agitation whose influence extends to the heart."

Closer to the twentieth century, some prominent physicians were beginning to identify, in addition to the intense emotional states and their acute effects described thus far, a relationship between heart disease and more enduring personality traits. In 1868 the German physician T. von Deusch described the coronary-prone person as one who has the practice of often working through the night and speaking in a loud voice.

Sir William Osler, an American who became distinguished professor of medicine at Oxford University during the early years of this century, provided us with a number of keen insights regarding associations between the emotional side of life and afflictions of the heart. He described the typical coronary patient as ". . . not the delicate, neurotic person . . . but the robust, the vigorous in mind and body, the keen and ambitious man, the indicator of whose engine is always at 'full speed ahead.' " Osler attributed the development of coronary heart disease to ". . . the high pressure at which men live and the habit of working the machine to its maximum capacity."

In describing the sorts of circumstances likely to bring on attacks of anginal chest pain, Osler said, "Mental worry, severe grief, or a sudden shock may precede directly the onset of the attacks." As with Mary Smith in chapter 1, Osler described one patient in whom the paroxysms came on after the shock of the announcement that a son had committed suicide.

And so we have come full circle. These observations and stories make a strong case that the mind and the emotions *can* affect the heart, and that such effects have the capacity to cause heart disease, even death. But this sort of circumstantial evidence, based as it is on anecdotal observations, even by such a giant as Osler, provides no more than good clues to the causal agents for any disease; it could never constitute proof of causality. Sure, Ananias and Sapphira died when chastised by Peter, and so did Sir John Hunter after the stormy board meeting; but what about all the people who are chastised and don't die? Or who engage in heated arguments and don't die?

Friedman and Rosenman realized the need to go beyond circumstantial evidence, to go from anecdote to epidemiology—and began their more systematic research to document the role of Type A behavior in coronary heart disease.

THE EMERGENCE
OF THE TYPE A CONCEPT

Besides the historical precedents described above, when Friedman and Rosenman began their work in the 1950s, a number of studies had already been published by psychiatrists wherein small numbers of patients with coronary disease were compared to healthy people or to patients with some other disease. These studies identified several traits as more common in the heart attack patients, including aggressive tendencies, anger and hostility, and striving for power and achievement.

When they considered these earlier findings in the light of their own extensive experience in caring for patients with coronary disease, Friedman and Rosenman became convinced that a certain constellation of behavioral traits was uniformly more likely to be present in their patients with coronary disease than in other persons who were free of disease. These characteristics included: (1) almost obsessive attempts to achieve many poorly defined goals, (2) love of competition, (3) a strong need for recognition and advancement, (4) a consistent preoccupation with time and the need to get things done in a hurry, (5) intense concentration and alertness, and (6) high levels of "free-floating hostility."

They next formulated the hypothesis that this set of behavioral traits is a risk factor for coronary heart disease. The basis for this initial proposal could best be understood as "guilt by association": since most heart attack victims displayed these traits, while healthy persons did not, then these traits must play a role in causing the heart attacks.

This line of reasoning was not unlike that which began the research leading to the conclusion that elevated blood cholesterol is a risk factor for coronary disease. In the late nineteenth century, the German pathologist Rudolf Virchow noted that most patients who had had angina prior to a sudden demise had yellowish deposits in the coronary arteries supplying blood to the heart muscle. Analysis of these deposits showed that they were loaded with cholesterol. Just as with Friedman and Rosenman's observation of the frequent presence of their set of behavioral traits in heart attack victims, the presence of these cholesterol-containing deposits led Virchow and others to the hypothesis that these were somehow causing the illness that had killed those in whom they were so often found at postmortem examination—guilt by association.

But such associations do not prove causation. Any factor commonly found in persons suffering from a given disease can just as easily be a *result* as a cause of that malady. For example, persons with a slipped disk almost always complain of pain and, if the problem continues, appear depressed. This does not mean, however, that pain and depression cause the disk to be ruptured; quite the opposite. What comes *first* is most likely to be the causal factor.

So, before the medical community could conclude that high blood cholesterol is a risk factor for coronary disease, it was necessary to show that the elevated blood cholesterol preceded the appearance of the coronary disease—and this is precisely what the Framingham study accomplished. For the same reasons, Friedman and Rosenman had a lot of work to do before their hypothesized set of coronary-prone behavioral traits could be accepted as a coronary risk factor.

The first step was to give it a name. After several failures to obtain federal funding for research on a "coronary-prone personality," Friedman and Rosenman were advised by a scientist at the National Institutes of Health to use some term that did not convey any theoretical meaning—a term, in other words, that would not draw the wrath of those scientists with specific theoretical biases who were reviewing their funding applications. Hence the birth of the now famous appellation, "Type A behavior." To describe those persons who did not have the characteristics making up the Type A pattern, they simply used the term "Type B."

Before Friedman and Rosenman could establish it as a coronary risk factor, they first had to devise a reliable means of measuring the Type A behavior pattern. For the cholesterol research, this had been relatively simple, since a biochemical assay gave exact, "objective" numerical information regarding how much cholesterol was in the blood. To measure a set of behaviors was not so simple, however.

The standard means of measuring personality traits in psychology is the questionnaire. By studying a person's responses to an array of self-report questions, one may derive numerical measures of certain traits, such as extroversion (outgoingness) and neuroticism (high emotionality). Friedman and Rosenman rejected this approach. They felt that Type A persons were not very aware of the presence of their Type A characteristics and would not be able, or willing, to give accurate and reliable answers on a questionnaire.

This potential problem led Friedman and Rosenman to develop a structured interview as the standard means of measuring Type A behavior; a method that also enabled them to focus on speech characteristics that they felt would mark the Type A person, even when his overt answers did not appear to be Type A. Thus, if one responds to the question, "Do you rush and hurry in doing most things?" before it is even finished, saying in a loud, staccato voice, "Hell no! I *never* allow outside demands to rule *me!,*" we would conclude that the content of the answer is Type B. The manner in which the answer is delivered, however, clearly portrays a very Type A outlook.

Now in possession of a tool for the reliable measurement of Type A behavior, Friedman and Rosenman carried out a number of preliminary studies to confirm their clinical impression that most of their heart attack patients displayed high levels of ambition, time urgency, loud and accelerated speech, free-floating hostility, and the like—in other words, were "Type A."

The results of these studies were promising. Male heart attack victims were indeed more often assessed as Type A in comparison to healthy persons and patients with other health problems. Even among women, those whom their friends described as Type A were more likely to already have some manifestation of coronary disease. Further studies linked Type A behavior to higher blood cholesterol levels, strengthening the case that Type A behavior could lead to coronary disease.

One study during this early period was particularly interesting. It demonstrated that when environmental circumstances elicit Type A behavior bodily changes occur, leading to increased coronary disease risk. On a regular basis, a group of accountants reported to San Francisco's Mt. Zion Hospital, where Drs. Friedman and Rosenman carried out their research and where the group gave blood samples that were analyzed for cholesterol level. These levels were not stable across the year, but varied in ways that indicated that environmental demands to accomplish more and more things in less and less time—in other words, to behave in a more Type A way—have an effect on blood cholesterol levels that could contribute to increased risk of heart attack. The cholesterol levels were generally low and stable during most of the year, with two exceptions: There were sharp increases in cholesterol levels during the weeks leading up to the January 1 and April 15 tax deadlines.

So far, so good, but still circumstantial. Still, besides convincing Friedman and Rosenman of the correctness of their hypothesis, the evidence they had collected allowed them to make a persuasive case for the definitive test, a prospective study that would seek to *predict* these occurrences. In fact, they were successful in obtaining a large grant from the National Institutes of Health for that purpose, to conduct the Western Collaborative Group Study.

This pioneering study demonstrated a *prospective* relationship between a proposed risk factor, in this case Type A behavior, and increased *subsequent* risk of suffering some manifestation of coronary heart disease.

Beginning in the early 1960s, over 3,000 men between the ages of 39 and 59 who were free of any evidence of coronary disease were enrolled in the study and carefully followed for eight and a half years. The doctors sought to determine who developed any manifestations of coronary heart disease, including a heart attack requiring hospitalization, angina pectoris (chest pain due to coronary arterio-sclerosis), a "silent" heart attack (changes on the electrocardiogram indicating a heart attack had occurred, but no memory of chest pain or other symptoms on the patient's part), or death due to coronary disease.

At the start of the study, the structured interview was used to determine who was Type A and who was Type B, and all of the traditional risk factors were carefully assessed as well. The structured interview was repeated for some of the men after one year and was found to be quite stable. About half the men were classified as Type A, half Type B.

The results of the Western Collaborative Group Study confirmed the risk factors identified in the Framingham Study: those who at the start of the study had high blood pressure, had high cholesterol levels, or were cigarette smokers were significantly more likely to develop coronary disease than those without these risk factors. Also confirming the Framingham results: the more risk factors present, the higher the risk. Thus, two risk factors were predictive of coronary event rates more than twice those associated with one risk factor. Three risk factors predicted still higher disease rates.

While these results were important in both confirming the Framingham results in a sample of similar size and showing that the known risk factors were indeed acting as expected in the Western Collaborative Group Study, the main question was the Type A hypothesis—would the approximately 1,500 Type A men have more coronary events? As shown in Figure 2-1, by the end of the 8½-year follow-up, the men who were Type A at the start of the study were about twice as likely as their Type B counterparts to have suffered some manifestation of coronary disease. This increased risk held up even when specific categories of heart problems were considered—Type As had more overt heart attacks, more silent heart attacks, more angina, more

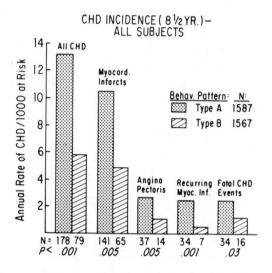

2-1. Coronary heart disease (CHD) rates during an 8½-year follow-up period for Type A and Type B men in the Western Collaborative Group Study. (Reprinted with permission from *Annals of Clinical Science*, 1971, vol. 3, p. 305.)

deaths, and even more second heart attacks among those who had had a first heart attack after the start of the study.

Although skepticism had greeted Friedman and Rosenman's initial research on the Type A hypothesis, *these* results could not be dismissed so easily. While some had argued earlier that a heart attack could itself make one more irritable, more in a hurry to accomplish his goals now that his life span might be shortened, it was far harder to explain away the new findings. Just as the Framingham Study showed for cholesterol, smoking, and high blood pressure, in the Western Collaborative Group Study the proposed risk factor, Type A behavior, had been assessed in healthy persons *prior* to any evidence of coronary disease. And, as with the established risk factors that emerged from Framingham, Type A behavior was also found to predict a significant increase in coronary risk over a comparable follow-up period.

The only criticism remaining suggested that Type A behavior predicted such an increased risk not because it was a bona fide independent risk factor, but because it was no more than a proxy for the already established risk factors. That is, this criticism claimed Type As went on to have more heart attacks simply because they were people more likely to smoke and have high blood pressure or high cholesterol levels in the first place. In fact, some even argued that since Type As did smoke more, the nicotine effects could actually have been responsible for the Type A behavior, and indirectly (via smoking's effect to raise coronary risk) for the Type A men's increased coronary risk as well. Sophisticated statistical analyses showed that none of the attempts to explain away the Type A finding could be supported. The Type A effect was entirely independent of the other risk factors. Indeed, among those with one or more of the traditional risk factors, the Type A men's disadvantage relative to Type Bs was even worse than in those men with no other risk factors.

The Western Collaborative Group Study was a signal success in achieving Friedman and Rosenman's goal of demonstrating that Type A behavior is—just like cholesterol, smoking, and high blood pressure—an *independent* coronary risk factor. The scientific skepticism began to wane, and even the American public began to take note of Type A behavior, especially following the publication, in 1974, of Friedman and Rosenman's widely read book, *Type A Behavior and Your Heart*. Movie characters cursing the rush hour traffic or upbraiding a clumsy waiter might be told by a companion, "Stop being so Type A!" Magazine cartoons began to appear, depicting Type A behavior in an array of situations, even encompassing Type A dogs and cats. Sometime in the mid-1970s, the term *Type A* entered the American lexicon.

Besides its impact on American culture, the Western Collaborative Group Study results had some other benefits. The excitement generated by Friedman and Rosenman's innovative research—applying standard, accepted epidemiologic research techniques to the evaluation of a fuzzy psychological concept, and succeeding—attracted, from the early 1970s on, a growing cadre of young researchers from a number of different scientific disciplines, including psychologists, sociologists, anthropologists, internists, cardiologists, pharmacologists, and others. These new researchers might best be termed the "second generation" to work on the Type A hypothesis.

THE TYPE A HYPOTHESIS: SECOND-GENERATION RESEARCH

I was one of those enticed by the new research possibilities indicated by a mind-body phenomenon that had actually been demonstrated to be "real." Since medical-school days I had been interested in psychosomatic medicine and had even done some research showing that interviews about personal topics raised blood pressure levels more in patients with high blood pressure already than in patients with other diseases. The problem I faced was the same as that I described earlier: how to prove causation (in this case that high blood pressure is caused by larger blood pressure responses) when the evidence is only circumstantial.

But here were Friedman and Rosenman with a completed study of healthy men that had actually worked, had actually shown that a psychological factor *predicted* increased risk of a disease. I realized there were some other advantages to studying coronary heart disease. In contrast to high blood pressure, where the underlying "lesion," or pathological change in the body's tissues responsible for the disease, was unknown, in coronary disease there was an actual lesion that could be observed in living people—the arteriosclerotic plaque in the coronary arteries. Though we still don't understand fully all of the processes involved in the development of these plaques (a fuller discussion of what we do know will be presented later), they at least exist to be measured and evaluated when the appropriate diagnostic studies are done.

Thus, research not only could investigate the development of symptoms in association with a psychological factor (Type A behavior), but also could evaluate the relationship of that factor to the actual tissue changes (arteriosclerotic plaques) that underlie those symptoms. Also encouraging to me was the fact that Friedman and Rosenman (whose early research anticipated much of what has come along since) had already published a paper in which they reported the results of postmortem examination of the coronary arteries of those men in the Western Collaborative Group Study who died during the follow-up period. They revealed there were more severe arteriosclerotic blockages of the coronary arteries among the Type A men who had died than among the deceased Type B men.

Recognizing the opportunity to conduct exciting research in the Type A area, not long after I joined the Department of Psychiatry faculty at Duke in 1972, I visited Friedman and Rosenman in San Francisco and learned how to use their structured interview method to assess Type A behavior.

At this point the only question was how to start my investigation—on what aspect of the Type A hypothesis should I focus? The answer came in the form of James Blumenthal, a psychology graduate student who needed a research topic for his Ph.D. dissertation and wanted to do something in the psychosomatic area. "Why not," I suggested, "see if, among those patients in whom our cardiologists are doing coronary arteriograms, the Type As have

more severe arteriosclerosis?" If they did, this would suggest that Type A behavior not only caused more heart
attacks and deaths, as Friedman and Rosenman had already
found, but also was involved in forming the underlying
pathological lesion in the coronary arteries of heart attack
victims.

Blumenthal liked the idea, and within a few days we
had visited the head of our cardiac catheterization lab and
secured his help in providing Jim with access to the patients. Then as now, the major reason for doing coronary
arteriography was to determine the number and size of
arteriosclerotic blockages present in the coronary arteries.
The coronary arteriogram procedure involves inserting a

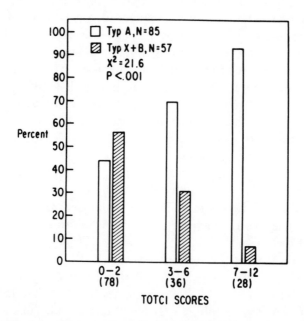

2-2.   Type A and coronary arteriosclerosis—proportions of Type A and
Type X or B patients at Duke in groups with mild (TOTCI Scores =
0–2), moderate (TOTCI = 3–6), and severe (TOTCI = 7–12) coronary
arteriosclerosis as documented by coronary arteriography. (Reprinted
with permission from *Circulation*, 1978, vol. 258, p. 637.)

tube in an artery and advancing it up to the heart, where it is inserted into the coronary arteries that provide the blood supply to the heart muscle. There, a dye solution is injected, and X-ray pictures are taken that give a view of the inside of the arteries. Arteriosclerotic blockages show up as defects in the smooth tubular shape of the artery. If such blockages are present, the patient might be treated with surgery to "bypass" the blockage with a vein transplanted from his leg.

Within the span of a year, Jim had done Type A structured interviews on 142 patients who had undergone the arteriographic examination. His results were as predicted and quite striking. As shown in Figure 2-2, among those patients with few or no arteriosclerotic blockages in their coronary arteries, about half were Type A and half were Type B. Among those with more severe blockages, over 70 percent were Type A; and among those with very severe blockages (at least two major arteries totally shut down), over 90 percent were Type A.

Good research ideas often occur to scientists at different sites at the same time. While Jim was doing his interviews at Duke, investigators at Columbia University and at Boston University were carrying out similar studies. It was gratifying to Jim and me to learn that their results closely paralleled ours: in both cases the Type A patients had more severe coronary arteriosclerosis than the Type Bs.

Few experiences are more satisfying to the scientist than having important findings replicated by colleagues at other institutions. It means that what you found is likely to be true, and not just some fluke or, even worse, the result of some mistake on your part. This experience has been described as almost (but not quite!) like finding out that the one you love loves you.

At this point, during the spring and early summer of 1975, Friedman, Rosenman, and those of us who had followed in their footsteps had ample reason to feel a satisfying sense of accomplishment, of a job well done. The early anecdotal observations had led to the prospective Western Collaborative Group Study and it was found that Type As were twice as likely to develop coronary disease as Type Bs. The studies of patients undergoing coronary arteriography were unanimous in showing that Type As had more severe levels of coronary arteriosclerosis. Laboratory research (see chapter 5) was showing physiological responses in Type As that could help explain their more severe arteriosclerosis. Even a report from the Framingham Study itself, the "gold standard" source of our knowledge regarding coronary risk factors, corroborated these findings.

In light of all this exciting progress, it was clearly time to make a "statement" to the medical community. Accordingly, with the encouragement and support of Dr. Stephen Weiss, Dr. Mary Jane Jesse, and others at the National Heart, Lung, and Blood Institute (NHLBI), Dr. Theodore Dembroski organized and hosted a meeting in St. Petersburg, Florida, in the spring of 1977 that was attended by most of those doing Type A research. The proceedings of this meeting contained all the currently available information, both published and unpublished, on the relationship between Type A behavior and coronary heart disease. Needless to say, although some areas were identified as needing further work, e.g., biological mechanisms and developmental aspects, the general conclusions were quite positive in presenting Type A behavior as a bona fide risk factor for coronary heart disease, a risk factor comparable in its impact to the other established risk factors of smoking, high cholesterol, and high blood pressure.

A subsequent meeting of scientists who had not participated in the St. Petersburg meeting or been associated with the Type A research was convened by the NHLBI a year later and agreed for the most part with these conclusions. Type A had finally arrived, or so we thought.

But there was trouble ahead.

THREE

EUPHORIA GIVES
WAY TO UNCERTAINTY

A s Thomas Kuhn notes in his book *The Structure of Scientific Revolutions,* new discoveries and theories in science are often resisted at first, even when existing paradigms are recognized to suffer from limitations. From the very beginning, Friedman and Rosenman's research on the Type A hypothesis was met with suspicion by many. Psychiatrists were concerned with an oversimplified classification that divided the human race into only two types, ignoring the underlying complexity of the human personality. At the same time, cardiologists were not prepared to accord risk-factor status to something as nebulous as a behavior pattern; to them, risk factors were *physical* things that had *physical* effects on the cardiovascular system. As we shall see, some of these concerns were eventually supported by such a wide array of adverse evidence that they could not be ignored or dismissed.

But first came the euphoria. Following the St. Petersburg conference and the subsequent acceptance of Type A as a coronary risk factor by a blue ribbon panel of scientists convened by the National Heart, Lung, and Blood Institute, the Type A hypothesis appeared to have triumphed. To be sure, there were some minor annoyances, such as a study from the Massachusetts General Hospital in Boston that had failed to find more severe arteriosclerosis in the coronary arteries of Type A as compared to Type B patients. But for the most part, it was full speed ahead with research to deepen our understanding of Type A behavior and its effects upon the heart.

The research community began to study the effects of Type A behavior on an even larger scale. A psychologist, David Jenkins, worked with Friedman and Rosenman to develop a paper-and-pencil test for Type A behavior. This questionnaire, the Jenkins Activity Survey, or JAS, was designed to provide a more objective measure, one not limited by the need for trained personnel to administer the structured interview, a test that could be used "off the shelf" by researchers around the world. Early results with the JAS were promising; a study at Boston University used the JAS to assess Type A behavior and found high JAS scores to correlate with more severe arteriosclerosis in the coronary arteries.

The early success of the Type A research also led other researchers in the late 1970s to incorporate Type A assessment into large-scale studies that had been designed for other purposes. By "piggybacking" Type A measurement into these very expensive (each one cost tens of millions of federal dollars to mount) ongoing studies, it would be possible at little additional cost to obtain further evidence as to how Type A relates to various aspects of coronary heart disease. Since it was short and easy to administer, the JAS was the logical instrument to assess Type A behavior in these studies.

One such study was the Aspirin Myocardial Infarction Study (AMIS), designed to see if aspirin therapy would prevent (by inhibiting blood clotting) further coronary disease problems in patients who had had a heart attack. Friedman and Rosenman's Western Collaborative Group Study had shown that Type A predicts heart attacks in healthy middle-aged men. The question posed in AMIS was whether Type A would predict later heart problems in patients who had already had a first heart attack.

Patients in this study completed the JAS at the start of the study and were then followed for several years. It was expected that those who tested as Type A on the JAS would have more problems during the follow-up period, but the results provided no support for this hypothesis: JAS scores did not predict subsequent heart attacks, deaths, or other manifestations of coronary disease in these patients. Other large research studies raised similar suspicions.

Negative results in these studies caused much consternation among those committed to the Type A hypothesis. At first, we tended to fault the JAS. This paper-and-pencil questionnaire was probably not as good a measure of Type A behavior, we thought, as the "gold standard," the structured interview. Furthermore, the factors that predict how patients do once coronary disease is manifest may not be the same as those that predict the first event.

But no sooner had we publicly advanced these explanations than another major blow fell, one that could not be countered so easily. Ever since high blood pressure, elevated cholesterol levels, and smoking had been identified as coronary disease risk factors in the Framingham study, the National Heart, Lung, and Blood Institute had been planning to take the logical next step in applying these findings: a study that showed that if one reduces his risk factors, his risk of coronary disease also decreases. The hope was that such a demonstration would make an even stronger case in favor of a massive public health campaign to induce the

American population to treat its high blood pressure, to undertake whatever steps—dietary or medicinal—needed to lower its cholesterol levels, and to stop, or never start, smoking.

This study, the Multiple Risk Factor Intervention Trial (MRFIT), cost nearly one hundred million dollars before it was concluded. From 1973 to 1982, over 12,000 men, whose high blood pressure, cholesterol level, and smoking habit placed them at high risk for a heart attack, were enrolled in programs designed to reduce these risk factors: high blood pressure was treated, diet and drugs were employed to reduce cholesterol levels, and an intensive behavior modification program was initiated to induce the men to give up smoking.

As with the AMIS and other studies, the earlier success of the Type A research led the MRFIT team to incorporate a further test of the Type A hypothesis into their study. In contrast to the AMIS and other studies, however, this would be a test in healthy men; though they had elevated coronary risk factors, the MRFIT men had not yet had a heart attack. Thus, it was thought this sample group would provide a more accurate test of whether the Western Collaborative Group Study results could be replicated in an independent study.

To provide an even closer reproduction of the Friedman and Rosenman approach in their prospective study, the MRFIT researchers used the structured interview as well as the JAS as a measure of Type A in a subset of about 3,000 men. To ensure that the interviews were properly performed, Dr. Rosenman himself trained the interviewers as well as auditors who also listened to the interviews to confirm the Type A assessments. Whenever the auditors disagreed on the Type A classification of any MRFIT participant, Dr. Rosenman made the final determination of Type A status.

Thus, in nearly every respect the Type A subproject

of the MRFIT study would be comparable to the original Western Collaborative Group Study's design. The number of men to be studied was about the same; the assessment of Type A was done with the same approach, even employing Dr. Rosenman to monitor the interviews; and the follow-up period was comparable. The only different thing was that all the men in the MRFIT study had elevated risk factors, whereas the men in the Western Collaborative Group Study had not been selected for that reason. Further analyses of the Western Collaborative Group Study data had shown, however, that Type A predicted increased coronary risk, if anything, even better in those men with increased traditional risk factors. Therefore, the high-risk aspect of the MRFIT sample was not expected to affect its validity in testing the Type A hypothesis.

Despite this, and much to the surprise of the MRFIT team, when the final results were in, no relationship was discernible between Type A behavior and any of the coronary disease endpoints. This was important, deeply distressing news to the Type A research community.

During this period, the late 1970s and early 1980s, also coming to light were several additional studies of Type A behavior in patients undergoing coronary arteriography. I described three such studies in the last chapter (in which increased coronary arteriosclerosis was found in the Type A patients). Since then, approximately ten similar studies have been performed. In only two of these was any measure of Type A behavior found to correlate with more severe coronary arteriosclerosis. Eight of the ten studies failed to confirm the Type A hypothesis.

Combined with the findings of the MRFIT and other prospective studies, these results only added to the state of confusion, some would say disarray, regarding the current status of the Type A hypothesis. Was Type A a risk factor or wasn't it? How could the conflicting results of the various studies be explained? In a 1985 *New England Journal of*

Medicine editorial on the subject, Dr. Marcia Angell concluded, "The evidence for mental state as a cause and cure
of today's scourges is not much better than it was for the
afflictions of earlier centuries." In other words, according
to Dr. Angell, the Type A hypothesis and other proposals
that psychological factors play a role in the causation of
human disease were "largely folklore."

Negative results continued to mount disturbingly.
Even the Western Collaborative Group Study itself was
recently used to question the Type A hypothesis. In a January 1988 issue of the *New England Journal of Medicine,* we
learned that among the 231 men in the Western Collaborative Group Study who had had a heart attack and survived
beyond the first twenty-four-hour period, the Type As had
a significantly *better* long-term survival! Thus, not only
were Type As not at increased risk of dying following a
heart attack, but during a twenty-two-year follow-up period, their death rate was only 58 percent that seen among
the Type Bs. This, too, was difficult to explain, and only
added to the already increasing uncertainty surrounding
Type A research, as well as coronary disease prevention
and treatment techniques.

At first I didn't accord the negative studies much
weight. In my own research at Duke, the JAS had not
correlated with arteriosclerosis severity, but I simply concluded that the negative studies that used the JAS assessment for Type A could not be accepted as definitive. It also
seemed to me that I and other researchers trying to understand the role of human behavior in coronary heart disease
and other ailments were getting more than our share of
attacks in professional journals and the general press.

Still, although I was not convinced these criticisms
were completely justified, my own thinking was slowly
becoming influenced by the negative studies—after all,
even if some of them could be dismissed as flawed, their
sheer number meant the findings could not be entirely

discounted. And some, such as the MRFIT study, were based on what I knew was meticulously conducted research.

Eventually, even my own research at Duke began to reveal disconcerting weaknesses in the relationship between Type A behavior and coronary arteriosclerosis. When we examined the relationship between Type A behavior (as assessed by the structured interview) and coronary arteriosclerosis in over 2,200 patients who had undergone the coronary arteriographic diagnostic procedure at Duke between 1976 and 1980, it became clear that Type A alone was surely not the best we could do in defining coronary-prone behavior.

As shown in Figure 3-1, there remained a significant relationship between Type A and coronary arteriosclerosis, but it varied as a function of age. Among our younger patients, those below age 50, the Type As did have, as predicted, more severe arteriosclerosis. Among the patients over age 55, however, the picture was quite different: In that group, the *Type Bs* had more severe disease.

Such a reversal could be explained by the operation of *survival effects*. That is, among the younger patients the Type As had, as expected, more severe disease. But the older Type A patients were of a different order, perhaps; they were survivors, hardy people who had not succumbed to coronary disease earlier in life.

So, when is a "risk factor" not a risk factor? When those who are susceptible to it have all died off, leaving only the hardier, resistant ones in the population to study. That is how the Framingham researchers, who identified the survival effect at work in their own study, explain the marked weakening of smoking and high cholesterol levels as coronary risk factors with advancing age, and it seemed a reasonable explanation for the paradoxical reversal of the relationship between Type A behavior and coronary arteriosclerosis we observed in our patients at Duke, too.

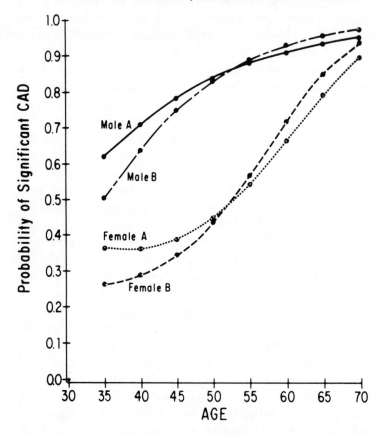

PROBABLITY OF AT LEAST ONE DISEASED VESSEL
BY SEX, AGE AND SI ASSESSMENT
ADJUSTED FOR SMOKING, CHOLESTEROL AND HYPERTENSION

3-1. Differing relation between Type A and coronary arteriosclerosis as a function of increasing age—proportions of Type A and Type B (as assessed using the structured interview: SI) patients at Duke with at least one coronary artery blocked by arteriosclerosis, shown as a function of age; male and female patients are shown separately. The relationships shown are statistically significant after statistical adjustment for the standard risk factors. (Reprinted with permission from *Psychosomatic Medicine*, 1988, vol. 50, p. 143.)

So far, so good, but we still had a problem. As shown in Figure 3-2, the relationship of cholesterol to arteriosclerosis also weakened with increasing age. But when examined among the younger heart patients, the impact on disease severity of having high cholesterol was much greater than the impact of Type A behavior. While the younger Type A patients were only 1.2 times more likely than the Type Bs to have a severe arterial blockage, those younger patients with high cholesterol levels were *twice* as likely to have a severe blockage as those with low cholesterol levels.

This indicated to me that Type A was not a very strong risk factor, not only in all the negative studies described earlier, but even in my own research. There was *something* there, but I was left with the gnawing feeling that Type A was not the most precise way of describing what psychological element was actually toxic to the coronary arteries. Dr. Joel Dimsdale put it well in a 1988 *New England Journal of Medicine* editorial:

> It is important to acknowledge that *something* is going on in terms of the relation between personality and heart disease. However, the nature of that influence is far more complex than is conveyed by the simple assertion that Type A behavior is a risk factor for coronary heart disease.

Fortunately, by the time I reached this conclusion our research had already begun to provide some exciting clues as to the nature of that something. As you will recall, Friedman and Rosenman's original description of the Type A pattern included a sense of time urgency, high levels of ambition and striving for achievement, and free-floating hostility. Following their lead, we had all simply accepted, more or less as gospel, the proposition that all of these

PROBABILITY OF AT LEAST ONE DISEASED VESSEL
BY SEX, AGE AND CHOLESTEROL LEVEL
ADJUSTED FOR SI ASSESSMENT, SMOKING STATUS AND HYPERTENSION

3-2. Differing relation between cholesterol level and coronary arteriosclerosis as a function of increasing age—instead of Type A and B as in
Figure 3-1, patients (same ones as shown in Figure 3-1) are categorized
according to cholesterol level, whether high or low. (Reprinted with
permission from *Psychosomatic Medicine*, 1988, vol. 50, p. 146.)

elements were required for someone to be Type A and thus "coronary-prone."

I cannot tell you precisely when I began to question this proposition. Looking back, I know that I, like many others, found it hard to see why being ambitious should be so harmful; or even being in a hurry, for that matter. Hostility, on the other hand—well, it didn't take much imagination to see that aspect of Type A as something that, at the least, *should* be harmful.

I *can* tell you that by the 1977 conference in St. Petersburg I was almost sure that hostility held the key to understanding what was harmful about Type A behavior. I remember having as one of my research goals at the time to "do away" with Type A and substitute a more precise term—hostility, I was beginning to feel—for what was really coronary-prone about Type A.

This new, more specific focus on hostility was the critical shift in emphasis that enabled me, along with colleagues at other centers, to delineate which aspects of Type A behavior are harmful and which are not, thereby resolving some of the current uncertainty surrounding Type A's importance that the conflicting findings had generated.

All of this didn't happen overnight, however. It took several years of research and a lot of hard work by many people to gather the evidence needed to understand just how harmful hostility is. Let me tell you about it, so you will understand just how important it is to recognize hostility in yourself and those you care about so that, most important of all, you can begin to take those steps that will reduce the harm hostility will do in your life.

FOUR

ABOUT HOSTILITY AND TYPE A: FROM CONFUSION TO CLARIFICATION

John Smith (not his real name) was a self-made man who was used to getting his way—if he didn't, he'd let you hear about it. At age 44 he had already established his own successful service firm and was responsible for the payroll of over one hundred workers. In clawing his way up from the bottom, he had found that his fiery temper often contributed to his success: Most of those he dealt with learned soon enough that it did not pay to cross him.

All well and good until one fall afternoon, when Mr. Smith had the misfortune to be cut off by another car as he rushed from one job site to another. Ordinarily, he would have leaned on the horn and sped up "to pay the bastard back" within seconds of the provocation. But this time that didn't happen—just before his hand reached the horn, he felt as though a red-hot poker was being driven into the center of his chest. He couldn't catch his breath; he began to sweat all over, and within another few seconds, he felt sick to his stomach.

He pulled over to the side of the road and waited for the pain to subside. After two or three minutes it eased up some, but there was still an ache in the center of his chest and his left arm felt sore. He knew he'd better get to a doctor fast. He drove directly, but much more slowly than before, to Duke Hospital's emergency room, walked to the reception desk, and told the clerk there what had happened.

By the time an electrocardiogram (EKG) was set up, the pain was gone, and the EKG was perfectly normal. His symptoms alone were enough, however, to get him admitted to the coronary care unit with a presumptive diagnosis of a heart attack. The doctors wanted to see more EKGs over the next several days, as well as blood test results for heart muscle enzymes, to make sure he was not in mortal danger.

Over the next few days his EKGs remained completely normal, as did his heart enzyme levels. There was no indication of a heart attack, or, for that matter, of any heart abnormality whatsoever. He even passed an exercise stress test with flying colors. His doctor was ready to discharge him when, on the morning he was to leave, a lab technician in training had trouble obtaining a blood sample from him.

She stuck him twice without success and was about to try a third time when Mr. Smith decided that he had had just about enough. He was about to let her and her supervisor have a piece of his mind when the red-hot poker hit his chest again. An intern was called and obtained an EKG immediately. The reading showed that Mr. Smith's heart muscle was not getting the blood it needed through the coronary arteries (they are called "coronary" because they circle the heart like a crown, or *corona*).

Here was clear-cut evidence that something was profoundly wrong with his heart. His doctor kept him in the

hospital and scheduled an emergency coronary arteriogram. A tube was threaded up through a leg artery to his
heart, where dye was injected into the major arteries supplying the heart while X-ray pictures were taken. The pictures showed that one of these large arteries was almost
completely blocked by an arteriosclerotic plaque (which I
will discuss in greater depth later).

Mr. Smith eventually underwent surgery to bypass
this blockage with a vein transplanted from his leg. But his
treatment wasn't over yet. In view of the dramatic way his
anger had precipitated his symptoms, and his long history
of this behavior (which was likely to contribute to future
heart problems), Mr. Smith was referred to me in hopes
that I could help him learn to curb his anger.

In talking with Mr. Smith, I found he had never
trusted his workers to do their jobs right, even to the extent
that he always double-checked them. His suspicions that
they were less competent than he required were usually
confirmed, and this often led to angry outbursts on his part
(like the one he made to the lab technician). But because the
consequences of his anger had been brought so unmistaka-
bly to his attention, rather than trying to justify his anger
(as hostile people often do), Mr. Smith was highly motiva-
ted to learn to curb that reaction, as well as to change the
attitudes that fueled it.

He did well in our behavior-modification program,
and I shall describe in later chapters how you might adapt
a similar program to curb your own hostility and anger. I
mention Mr. Smith's case now because his experience provided the kind of evidence that was leading many of us
working with heart patients to suspect that hostility and
anger might be the most toxic aspects of Type A behavior.

But one case, even one as dramatic as Mr. Smith's,
doesn't prove that hostility and anger are the only aspects
of Type A behavior that hurt the heart. Both to document
their harmful influence and to show that other aspects of

Type A behavior are not harmful, it was necessary to back-track and carry out more systematic research, and that is what a number of us proceeded to do.

Since the mid-1970s, several research groups have been focusing attention on the various components that together make up the global Type A pattern. Our goal is similar to that of the biochemists who earlier had learned to break down the total amount of fat circulating in the blood into its various constituent parts. In doing so, the lipid biochemists showed that not all cholesterol is "bad"; only that associated with low-density lipoprotein (LDL) increases risk of coronary disease. By contrast, the cholesterol associated with high-density lipoprotein (HDL) is "good"; that is, high HDL levels appear to *reduce* coronary disease risk. Thus our understanding of cholesterol's role as a coronary risk factor has been valuably refined.

It appeared that a similar situation might obtain for the collection of characteristics—time urgency, high ambition, and hostility—that Friedman and Rosenman clumped together under the name "Type A." Though they had not singled out any one aspect as more harmful, many of us realized that if, like cholesterol, some aspects of Type A are "good" (or, at least, not harmful) and some are "bad," then separate analysis of these parts could lead to more accurate prediction of coronary risk. And as the negative studies continued to mount, it occurred to many of us that perhaps the negative results stemmed from this possibility, that not all aspects of Type A behavior are equally toxic. If the nontoxic aspects were being given more weight than the toxic ones in assessing Type A behavior in the negative studies, it might explain why Type A failed to predict.

There were ample reasons to think hostility might be the aspect of Type A behavior responsible for prediction of disease. Of course, Friedman and Rosenman had already identified it as one of the key aspects. And their thinking had been guided by numerous earlier case reports describing high levels of hostility and anger in heart patients as compared to patients with other illnesses.

Perhaps another, less rational, reason for our focusing on the separate components of Type A behavior, and on hostility in particular, was the pragmatic sense that there is utility in some aspects of Type A behavior, like time urgency and ambition. If *all* aspects of Type A are bad for one's health, then to improve health, all must be changed. But if all Type As slow down, renounce ambition, and stifle a desire to rise to the top in their work, how will all the work get done? On the other hand, it was far more difficult to find redeeming virtues in hostility.

I also had the desire to support what Aldous Huxley once described as the "noble hypothesis": a hypothesis which, if proven true, would do more good for the human race than proving some other hypotheses. Surely it would do more good for humankind to show that being hostile is bad for health than to show that being quick and ambitious is harmful.

But good intentions alone are never enough to prove any hypothesis, no matter how noble. We had to produce some objective evidence to support the idea that of all the parts making up the Type A behavior pattern, only those aspects related to hostility are toxic. The work required to confirm the "hostility hypothesis" began about 1974 and continues today. In the process, we have learned a great deal more about the nature of hostility and its relation to health and disease.

The first requirement to be filled was to determine some way of measuring hostility. Ultimately, two measurement tools were developed whose independent usages have now led us to the same general conclusion: Of all the characteristics grouped under the name Type A, *only those concerned with hostility and related characteristics are toxic to the heart.*

1974–83: HOSTILITY
MEASURED BY QUESTIONNAIRE

The first tool that helped us to pinpoint hostility was a questionnaire that Dr. Jim Blumenthal selected back in 1974 to use in his dissertation research, which, you will recall, found that Type As had more severe blockages of their coronary arteries.

As a result of our early discussions in planning his research, and his extensive preparatory reading, Jim felt it would be worthwhile to get some measures of hostility, in addition to the Type A interviews, on the patients he would be studying. I encouraged him to look further into the possibilities, and, taking into account a number of considerations, he chose to use fifty questions from the Minnesota Multiphasic Personality Inventory (MMPI) that two psychologists, Cook and Medley, had grouped into a "Hostility" (Ho) scale in 1954.

Before I go on to tell you what we found using the Cook and Medley Ho scale, a word is in order about the MMPI itself, because it's important to our story later. The MMPI is the most widely used psychological test ever developed. It consists of 550 different questions to which the person taking the test simply answers, usually by marking a space on an answer sheet, *True* or *False*. Developed over forty years ago to diagnose various forms of mental illness, such as schizophrenia and depression, the wide variety of content covered by the large number of items on the test has led psychologists over the years to use various combinations of these items to make new scales that measure any number of psychological traits. We'll come back to consider what the Ho scale evaluates, but now let me relate what we learned when we measured it in the Duke heart patients.

The first thing we found in Dr. Blumenthal's study

was that there was a strong tendency for those patients with high Ho scores to have more severe arteriosclerotic blockages in their coronary arteries. Although we never published this finding, I did present it at the 1977 meeting of Type A researchers in St. Petersburg, and I believe many of those present were stimulated to think more seriously about hostility as a result.

Another outgrowth of our establishing a clear relationship between Ho scores and arteriosclerosis—as well, of course, as the broader Type A–arteriosclerosis relationship we had found—was that I was able to secure in 1976 a grant from the National Heart, Lung, and Blood Institute to explore further the role of psychological and social factors in various aspects of coronary heart disease.

The plan of this research was to have patients undergoing coronary arteriography at Duke fill out a number of questionnaires and also undergo a structured interview to measure Type A behavior. A key part of the battery of questionnaires we used was the MMPI, mainly because it contained the Cook and Medley Ho scale that we had already found to correlate with arteriosclerosis, but also because it measured psychological problems, like depression, that often befall heart patients.

It did not take us long to do Type A interviews with over 400 patients and have them fill out the MMPI. The cardiologists examined the coronary arteriogram for each of these patients and determined how many coronary arteries had blockages.

When we compared our interview and questionnaire measures with the cardiologists' arteriogram readings, we focused first on the relationship of Type A behavior, as measured by the interview, to arteriosclerosis. It was reassuring to find again, confirming Jim Blumenthal's earlier results, that Type A patients were significantly more likely to have a major blockage of at least one artery.

Next we turned our attention to the Ho scale. It was

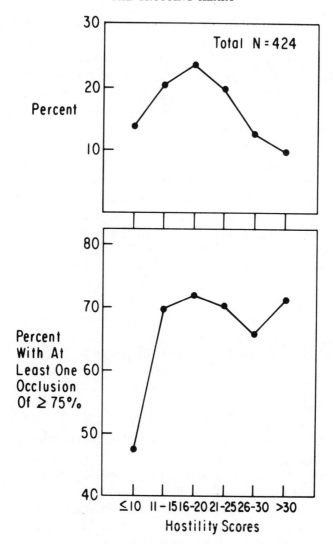

4-1. Relationship in 424 Duke patients between scores on the Cook and Medley Hostility (Ho) scale and likelihood of having one or more blocked coronary arteries, as shown in the bottom graph (the top graph shows the proportions of patients with each level of Ho score). (Reprinted with permission from *Psychosomatic Medicine*, 1980, vol. 42, p. 544.)

an even stronger predictor of coronary artery blockages than Type A behavior itself. As you can see in Figure 4-1, among patients with low Ho scores—10 or less out of a possible 50, signaling low hostility levels—only 48 percent had a major blockage in at least one coronary artery. In contrast, among the patients scoring higher than 10, about 70 percent were afflicted with at least one major blockage. Whereas Type As were 1.3 times more likely than non-As to have a major blockage, those patients with higher Ho scores were *1.5* times more likely to have severe disease.

To further refine our understanding of what was at work here, we did additional statistical tests that asked the question: Which is the stronger predictor of arteriosclerosis severity, Ho score or Type A? When we controlled for Ho scores in these analyses, the statistical significance of the Type A–arteriosclerosis relationship nearly disappeared. In marked contrast, when we controlled for Type A, the relationship of Ho scores to arteriosclerosis became even stronger. In our 1980 *Psychosomatic Medicine* paper describing these results, we concluded that hostility as measured by the Ho scale is at least as strong a predictor of coronary blockages as Type A itself, and probably accounted for some of the relationship between Type A behavior and coronary disease in our patients.

This was the first demonstration that a measure of hostility was associated with coronary disease more strongly than Type A behavior itself, and that this stronger association of hostility to disease held up even when Ho scores and Type A were compared head to head.

It was at this time, shortly after our paper describing these results was published in 1980, that the advantage of using a hostility scale from the MMPI became even more evident to us.

What we had found was an *association* between Ho scores and coronary disease. As we noted earlier with respect to Friedman and Rosenman's initial work on Type A, "association does not prove causation." Just as Friedman and Rosenman had to do a *prospective* study (showing that prior to any manifestation of disease, Type A was predicting eventual disease), if we wanted to make a strong case that hostility as measured by the Ho scale was *causing* disease, we would need to do a similar prospective study—seeing if Ho scores obtained prior to disease appearance predicted which persons would become ill.

While it would have been very expensive and time consuming to start a *new* prospective study for this purpose, the fact that the fifty Ho scale items were part of the long-used MMPI made it possible to accomplish the same thing at far less cost, and without having to wait.

Not long after the publication of our 1980 paper, Dr. Richard Shekelle wrote to me indicating his interest in seeing if the Ho scale *predicted* heart problems in the Western Electric Study. Back in the 1950s, Dr. Shekelle and his colleagues at Northwestern University in Chicago began a study of over 1,800 middle-aged male employees at Western Electric's Hawthorne Works plant. Complete risk-factor information had been obtained and a number of psychological tests administered, including the MMPI, in the late 1950s. Since that time, these men had been closely followed and all major illnesses and deaths had been carefully documented.

Now, in 1980, Dr. Shekelle would be able to go back and rescore for the Ho scale from the MMPIs obtained in the 1950s to see if they predicted heart problems over the ensuing decades.

Needless to say, I wrote back immediately that I thought his idea was splendid, sent him information on how to score the Ho scale, and asked him to please let me know as soon as possible what he found. A few months later a letter arrived from Dr. Shekelle. The analyses were

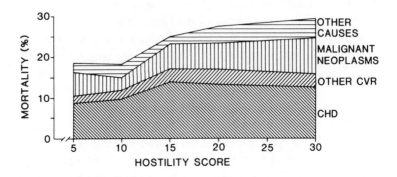

20-YEAR MORTALITY,

BY QUINTILE OF MMPI HOSTILITY SCORE,

WESTERN ELECTRIC STUDY, N=1877 MEN

4-2. Relation between Ho scores and risk of dying over a 20-year follow-up period in 1,877 middle-aged men who participated in the Western Electric Study. Causes of death are shown on the right ("CHD" = coronary heart disease; "OTHER CVR" = other cardiovascular-related). (Reprinted with permission from R.B. Williams, J.C. Barefoot and R.B. Shekelle, "The Health Consequences of Hostility," in M.A. Chesney and R.H. Rosenman, eds., *Anger and Hostility in Cardiovascular and Behavioral Disorders,* New York: Hemisphere, 1985, p. 178.)

nearly finished and Ho scores were indeed *predicting* increased risk of heart problems in the Western Electric workers.

Equally, if not more importantly, as you can see in Figure 4-2, not only deaths due to heart disease, but deaths due to *all* causes were markedly increased over a twenty-year follow-up period among those men whose Ho scores had been high back in 1957. Though cancer deaths were fewer in number than deaths due to heart disease, there was even a tendency for cancer deaths to increase as Ho scores went higher.

Since information was also available on these men's smoking habits, blood pressure, cholesterol level, and a variety of other possible risk factors, Dr. Shekelle and his associates were able to determine whether the prediction of heart problems or death by Ho scores could be accounted for by an association between Ho scores and higher levels of any risk factors. Indeed, those men with higher Ho scores did smoke more and consume more alcohol. But the analyses showed that these habits were not responsible for the increased health problems among the men with higher Ho scores.

Dr. Shekelle's news could not have been more encouraging for the "hostility hypothesis." He had extended our earlier finding of an *association* between high Ho scores and coronary arteriosclerosis to now include *prediction*, over a twenty-year follow-up period, of not only heart problems but deaths from any cause. Even the very shape of the relationship between Ho scores and the health measures in the two studies was remarkably similar, as you can see in comparing Figures 4-1 and 4-2. In Figure 4-1, those patients with Ho scores higher than 10 were about 1.5 times more likely to have a major artery blockage than those with scores of 10 or less. Similarly, in Figure 4-2, the twenty-year death rates among men whose Ho scores had been over 10 were about 1.5 times higher than those of men with Ho scores of 10 or less.

Sometime very soon after Dr. Shekelle's first letter, I learned from my research associate Thom Haney that Drs. John Barefoot and Grant Dahlstrom, psychologists at the University of North Carolina, ten miles down the road in Chapel Hill, were doing a follow-up study of 255 doctors who had taken the MMPI while in UNC Medical School twenty-five years ago. It did not take us long to meet and make plans to evaluate the twenty-five-year-old Ho scores as predictors of heart and other health problems in the UNC doctors.

The results were just as clear as those in Rick Shekelle's letter, with one important difference—the impact of Ho scores on heart problems and death rates was *even stronger*.

While the middle-aged Western Electric employees with higher Ho scores had been about 1.5 times more likely to develop heart problems or die than those with lower scores, the younger UNC physicians whose Ho scores had been higher twenty-five years ago were *four to five times more likely* to develop heart problems during the ensuing twenty-five years than those whose Ho scores had been lower.

The impact of Ho scores upon mortality was even more striking. In Figure 4-3 we see that only *2 percent* of those doctors with low Ho scores twenty-five years ago had died by the end of the twenty-five-year follow-up. In contrast, those with higher Ho scores experienced a *14 percent* mortality rate during the same period. In other words, those physicians with high Ho scores at age twenty-five were nearly *seven times more likely to die* by age 50 than those with low Ho scores. This provides us with a clearer picture of how survival effects work: Looking at Figure 4-3, it is not hard to see that by age 50 a lot more of the group with high Ho scores have died than those with low Ho scores. It is most likely that the 14 percent who died by age 50 were those with the most biological weaknesses, making it likely that the remainder of those with high Ho scores were hardier.

All this was dramatic news indeed. Even the established risk factors for coronary disease—smoking, high blood pressure, and high cholesterol—did not predict higher death rates than Ho scores did in this study. If confirmed in further research with large numbers of individuals, the impact on health, and on our sensibilities, of the trait measured by the Ho scale will definitely lead to a movement in favor of large-scale public health measures to reduce hostility. In the meanwhile, the available evidence is convincing (and those who wish to do something constructive about their own hostility will find some suggestions in part 2).

Recently, two additional studies appeared that failed

to find Ho scores predicting either heart problems or deaths due to all causes. Unlike the structured-interview assessment of Type A, where it is hard to discover after the fact why it may have failed to predict heart problems in the negative studies, with the psychometric approach embodied in the Ho scale approach, it is possible to understand some of the underlying reasons when it does not work as expected. In both the negative studies using the Ho scale, there were clear problems with the way in which the participants answered the Ho scale questions (see Sources and Notes). Thus, the failure of Ho scores to predict illness in these studies was not surprising.

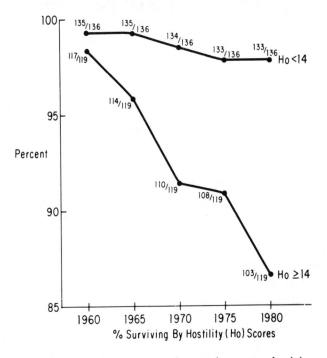

4-3. Differences in 25-year survival rates between physicians who scored low (less than 14) or high (14 or more) on the Ho scale during medical school. (Reprinted with permission from *Psychosomatic Medicine*, 1983, vol. 45, p. 61.)

Taken together, these findings indicate that something measured by the MMPI Ho scale is predicting not only heart disease, but also a wide variety of other serious health problems that emerge, sometimes causing death, later in life. Later, we shall consider what exactly that "something" is.

But first, let's look at the next step that helped confirm the so-called hostility hypothesis.

1974–85: HOSTILITY MEASURED BY THE STRUCTURED INTERVIEW

About the same time—1981–83—that we and Dr. Shekelle and his group were publishing the results of the follow-up studies in the UNC doctors and the Western Electric employees, I got a call from a psychologist at Florida's Eckerd College, Dr. Ted Dembroski, that introduced us to a different but complementary technique for assessing hostility, the Type A structured interview.

The use of the structured interview to assess not only Type A behavior but its various components began with the efforts of Penn State psychologist Raymond Bortner in the early 1970s. He sought to develop a means of scoring separately the various behaviors displayed by someone undergoing the standardized structured interview originally developed by Friedman and Rosenman. By listening to the tape-recorded interviews from the Western Collaborative Group Study, Dr. Bortner rated several components of Type A behavior, including hostility, anger directed outward (toward others), speed of speaking, explosive voice modulation, rapid responding to the interviewer's questions, competitiveness on the job or in sports, and the like.

Following Dr. Bortner's untimely death in 1975, a research team led by Dr. Karen Matthews (now at the Uni-

versity of Pittsburgh) carried on his work and published a
paper in 1977 describing differences in components ratings
between the 62 men in the Western Collaborative Group
Study who had had a heart attack during the study period
and a control group of 124 men who remained healthy.
Several components, including, interestingly, hostility,
differentiated between the heart attack victims and the men
who remained healthy. Since no statistical analyses were
done to see which component was really the strongest predictor, we are left with only an impression from this study
that hostility, at least as measured during the structured
interview, is one of the Type A components that predicts
heart problems.

Over the intervening years, Dr. Dembroski developed
and refined this component scoring technique and found
that the hostility component predicted blood-pressure reactions of experimental subjects performing a laboratory
task while being challenged constantly to do better. Stimulated by this finding, by the earlier results of Dr. Matthews's analysis of the Bortner ratings, and by our work at
Duke with the Ho scale, Ted proposed that we link up for
a collaborative study.

He knew that for several years we had been adminis-
tering structured interviews to Duke patients undergoing
coronary arteriography. If I would send him tape-recorded
structured interviews from 150 of our patients, Ted—without knowing any of the arteriogram results—would score
these interviews using his innovative scoring technique.
Then we would compare our independent assessments, his
of the hostility and other Type A components and ours of
the arterial blockages.

The results were as we had predicted. The higher a
patient's hostility score, the more severe were his or her
coronary artery blockages. And just as with our finding (see
p. 39) that Type A predicted arterial blockages only in the
younger patients, as shown in Figure 4-4, the impact of

Ted's hostility ratings was far stronger in the younger patients in the sample of tapes we sent him. The impact of hostility on disease was also far stronger than that of Type A in our study. If you look back at Figure 3-1, you will see that among the younger patients the Type As were only about 1.2 times more likely to have a major arterial blockage than the Type Bs. In marked contrast, you can see in Figure 4-4 that younger patients rated by Ted as high on hostility were *three to four* times more likely to have severe blockages than those rated low on hostility.

As with our earlier study comparing Ho scores and Type A as predictors of disease severity in our patients, these results, using an entirely different approach to measuring hostility, confirmed our impression that hostility is more strongly related to coronary disease than is the global Type A measure.

Ted's study also provided some evidence that other aspects of Type A behavior are not only *not* related to disease, but may actually be protective. When the relationship of hostility to arteriosclerosis was statistically taken into account, a measure of Type A speech, Explosive Voice Modulation, became *negatively* associated with disease severity. The more explosive the voice, the *less severe* was the arteriosclerosis.

All of these findings Ted obtained by scoring the Type A components of Duke patients were confirmed when he performed similar ratings of interviews from patients originally tested by Dr. Joel Dimsdale of the Massachusetts General Hospital.

These findings strengthened the analogy between Type A and high cholesterol as coronary risk factors. We have already noted that both are more strongly associated with disease among younger persons. Now it even appears that Type A may be similar to cholesterol in another important respect: Just as some components of the blood cholesterol are good and some are bad, so also does it now begin

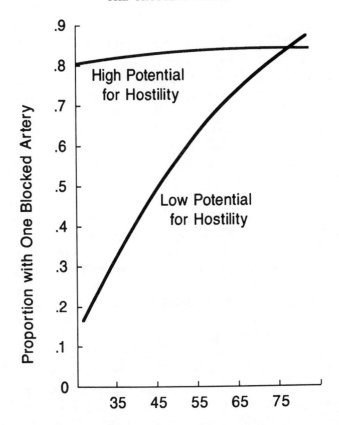

4-4. Differing relation between Potential for Hostility (rated from the structured interview tape recordings) and coronary arteriosclerosis as a function of increasing age (shown as the horizontal axis of the graph, and ranging from 35 to 75 in this group of 131 Duke patients). (Adapted from data originally published in *Psychosomatic Medicine*, 1985, vol. 47, pp. 219–33.)

to seem that some aspects of Type A may be good (vigorous speech, perhaps indicative of a positive, enthusiastic attitude) and some may be bad (hostility).

These findings, along with those we had obtained using the Ho questionnaire, suggested to us that most of the Type A assessments in the negative studies described in chapter 3 were not zeroing in on the toxic hostility component, but, rather, on other aspects, such as the rapid speech and time urgency characteristics, that our research was now showing to be nontoxic. If so, it would explain why such assessments failed earlier to reveal coronary risk accurately.

Additional evidence in favor of the hostility hypothesis came with reexamination of two earlier prospective studies—the Western Collaborative Group Study and the MRFIT study—that had used the structured interview to assess Type A behavior.

Following the earlier study reported by Dr. Matthews and colleagues in 1977, the remaining men in the Western Collaborative Group Study continued to be checked regularly to see who developed heart problems. Through the early 1980s, many other men in the sample were found to have developed coronary disease, making a total of 250 out of the original 3,000 men.

Drs. Margaret Chesney and Michael Hecker of the Stanford Research Institute reanalyzed—using a components scoring technique similar to Dr. Dembroski's—the interview tapes for these 250 men along with those from an additional 500 healthy men, similar in age and risk-factor status. As with the earlier study, the hostility component was a strong predictor of heart problems.

Their work went a step beyond the earlier study, however, using sophisticated "multivariate" statistical techniques to determine which Type A components were "independent" predictors. This enabled them to see not only which components were strong predictors, but also whether other components increased the prediction accuracy once the effects of the strongest components were considered.

The results were remarkably clear. Once the prediction of coronary problems by the hostility component was included in the predictive equation, *not a single other compo-*

nent added significantly to the prediction of heart disease. Dr. Dembroski independently confirmed these results using his scoring technique with the taped interviews from the same 750 men studied by Hecker and Chesney.

The evidence was mounting that only the hostility-related aspects of Type A behavior are toxic to the heart.

At this time, during the mid-1980s, Dr. Dembroski performed a similar analysis of taped interviews to compare those men in the MRFIT study who developed heart disease with a matched control group of men who remained healthy for the duration of the study. Remember, it was the failure of the interview-based assessments of Type A behavior to predict heart problems in the MRFIT study that had dealt the most severe blow to the acceptance of Type A as a means of defining coronary-prone behavior. If the hostility component could be shown to predict heart problems in the MRFIT men, it would provide very strong evidence that our hostility hypothesis was correct.

And indeed, the results of Ted's analysis of the MRFIT interviews were compelling: Those men scoring high on the hostility component at the start were about twice as likely to develop coronary heart disease during the follow-up period, compared to men with low hostility levels. As Hecker and Chesney had found in their assessment of the Western Collaborative Group Study interviews, no other component added significantly to the ability of the hostility component to predict heart problems in the MRFIT men.

Paralleling our earlier findings that both Type A and the hostility component were more strongly associated with arterial blockages in the younger patients, Dr. Dembroski found the hostility component was significantly more accurate in predicting coronary risk among the younger MRFIT men. Among those older than 47, the hostility component did not predict risk. These parallels increase our confidence in Ted's MRFIT findings.

During this same period, University of California at San Francisco psychologist Larry Scherwitz was using a somewhat different scoring approach to the structured interview. He had found earlier that blood-pressure reactions to lab stressors were larger among those who used more "self-references" during the structured interview. Thus, the more a person used the personal pronouns, "I," "me," "my," and "mine," the more his blood pressure rose when performing, say, a mental-arithmetic task. In subsequent studies Dr. Scherwitz found self-referencing both to correlate with disease severity and to predict heart problems, even in studies where Type A itself had failed to predict.

I believe these findings, using self-referencing and measures of hostility, are complementary: If one is hostile toward others, it is likely he will be more self-involved. The reasons for this will become clearer in a moment, for we shall turn now to a consideration of what the hostility measures are actually measuring.

1985–PRESENT: REFINING
THE DEFINITION OF HOSTILITY

Thus far, I have used the term *hostility* as though its meaning were perfectly clear and agreed upon by nearly everyone, scientist and layperson alike. One element of it is clear already: both the hostility component scored from the interview and scores on the Ho scale are measuring something that is certainly bad in terms of predicting more heart and other health problems.

Since the meaning of a concept like hostility can vary as a function of how it is measured, I think we need here to spend just a bit of time considering what actually is being assessed by the measurement techniques used in the research that has identified "hostility" as the toxic core of Type A behavior.

Not surprisingly, hostility, like Type A, has more than one dimension, whether it is assessed by interview technique or the Ho questionnaire. And it appears, also like Type A, that not all aspects of hostility are equally bad. This is important to recognize as we draw nearer to taking action to reduce the toll of hostility on our health.

In his rating of the hostility component using taped structured interviews, Dr. Dembroski based his judgments on the content, the intensity, and the style of responses to the interviewer's questions during the interview. Hostile *content* consisted of frequent reports of experiencing or expressing annoyance, irritation, resentment, anger, and the like, during the common frustrating circumstances of everyday life—e.g., lines that move too slowly at the bank or supermarket, people who seem to make a mess of every job they undertake. *Intensity* of hostility depended on the use of emotionally laden words, profanity, and voice emphasis—e.g., "I *hate* having to stand in lines that *creep* along! It makes me *mad* as *hell* to get stuck in lines!" A hostile *style* of interaction was indicated when the person being interviewed displayed rudeness, condescension, disagreeableness, and contempt in responding to the interviewer's questions—e.g., if the interviewee responded to the question, "When you get angry, do people around you know about it?" with something like, "What a stupid question! Of course they do, and if you keep asking me these silly questions, I'm gonna get up and leave!"

Drs. Cook and Medley designed their Ho scale to maximally differentiate between teachers who had good versus poor rapport with students. Not surprisingly, this led them to select fifty items that measure more than one aspect of one's psychological makeup.

Before we consider what they measure, we might note that Ho scores are very stable. Whether obtained from

entire MMPIs given years apart or from repeated administration of just the fifty Ho items themselves, the same persons will have virtually identical scores each time. This
stability suggests the trait(s) measured by the Ho scale may
be genetically determined, and several studies comparing
Ho scores in twins are now suggesting that genes probably
account for about 50 percent of the Ho score. Of course,
this means that 50 percent is also due to the environment,
so what happens to one can definitely influence how hostile
(as indicated by Ho scores) one becomes.

One time-honored way to tell what a psychological test
is measuring is to give the test along with a wide array of
other psychological tests to a large group of people and
then to look at how the other scales relate to the test in
which one is interested. This approach was taken by Dr.
Timothy Smith of the University of Utah. From the pattern of correlations he obtained, Dr. Smith concluded that
the Ho scale measures suspiciousness, resentment, frequent anger, and cynical mistrust of others. Persons with
high Ho scores also had scores on other tests suggesting
they were less hardy ("hardiness" reflects an enthusiastic,
"can do" approach to life), experienced more frequent and
severe hassles in everyday life, and derived little satisfaction from their everyday social contacts.

These characteristics have all been found to predict
health problems and may explain at least some of the poor
health found among persons with high Ho scores. In a
long-term study of nearly 7,000 citizens of Alameda
County, California, for example, researchers found that
people with fewer social ties—via marriage, contacts with
close friends and relatives, church membership, or membership in nonchurch groups—were two to three times
more likely to die from any cause than people who were
closely tied into social networks. It seems obvious to expect
that hostile persons would have fewer social ties—an expectation that is reinforced by a recent study we undertook
to clarify what the Ho scale measures.

In this study, we undertook a follow-up of 118 lawyers whose MMPIs—filled out in law school twenty-five years before—were providentially saved by Dr. Dahlstrom at UNC. We simply read the fifty Ho scale items and grouped them according to their surface content.

Dr. Kenneth Dodge, a Vanderbilt University psychologist specializing in the study of aggressive children, helped us read the Ho items and group them into these six categories:

Cynicism: a generally negative view of humankind, depicting others as unworthy, deceptive, and selfish; reflects beliefs regarding the behaviors of others toward the world in general, with the target of this behavior unspecified.

Hostile Attributions: a tendency to perceive others as intentionally trying to harm one; suspicion, paranoia, and fear of threat to self.

Hostile Affect: the experience of negative emotions in association with social relationships; admissions of anger, impatience, and loathing, when dealing with others; does not imply overt actions on the basis of the emotions.

Aggressive Responding: a tendency to use anger and aggression as a response to problems, or to endorse these behaviors as reasonable and justified; overt interpersonal behavior is indicated or implied.

Social Avoidance: admission that one avoids others; does not have the flavor of interpersonal confrontation contained in the other groups above.

Other: a miscellaneous category for items that do not fit any of the other groups' definitions.

With these definitions to follow, Dr. Dodge had fourteen psychologist colleagues read the Ho scale items and categorize each item into only one of the above six groups. Based on good agreement in assignments among this group

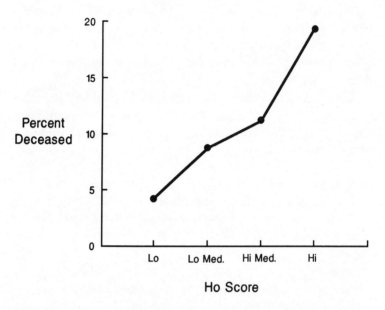

4-5. Relationship between Ho scores during law school and death rates over a 25-year follow-up period in 118 lawyers. (Adapted from data presented at the 1987 meeting of the American Psychosomatic Society.)

of psychologists, we had each of the fifty items assigned to only one group. The next task was to see whether scores on any of these groups predicted health outcomes better than the others.

Before doing that, it was essential that we knew first if the overall Ho score again predicted death due to all causes. As shown in Figure 4-5, we see that the prediction of deaths in these lawyers closely matched that which we had found earlier among the UNC physicians. Among those with lower Ho scores, the death rate in the twenty-five years following law school was less than 5 percent; in contrast, among those with higher scores, the death rate rose to 20 percent.

Reassured by this confirmation of our earlier Ho results in the doctors study, we moved ahead quickly, to see whether any of the six groups described above predicted mortality as well as, or better than the entire Ho scale score. Scores on the Hostile Attributions, Social Avoidance, and Other groups did not predict mortality at all. On the other hand, high scores on Cynicism, Hostile Affect, and Aggressive Responding did predict a significant increase in mortality rates.

In fact, each of these three latter groups was about as good a predictor of mortality as the entire Ho scale. And when we combined the items in these three groups into a single new scale, we had twenty-seven items—only about half of the fifty making up the entire Ho scale—reflecting a cynical and untrusting view of humankind, the frequent experience of negative emotions when dealing with others, and the frequent expression of overt anger and aggression when faced with frustration or problems. *The scores on this combined group of items predicted increased mortality far more reliably and strongly than did the entire Ho scale.*

A similar improvement in prediction of mortality was found when we applied scores on the same combined grouping of Ho items to the 255 physicians in our earlier study. This was very encouraging, suggesting that the improved prediction in lawyers was not some fluke.

What we had accomplished through this winnowing process of the Ho items might best be understood as a "distillation" of the toxic elements contained within the Ho scale. In essence, by grouping the items into the separate groups representing different aspects of hostility, we had achieved a separation of the elements making up the entire Ho scale into those that were toxic versus those that were not. Cynicism, Hostile Affect (i.e., anger), and Aggressive Responding are toxic, while the other groups of Ho items are not.

Taken together, these findings suggest that we are on the right track toward the ultimate goal of defining more and more precisely what aspects of hostility are leading to serious illnesses and death: a cynical mistrust of others that leads to the frequent experience of anger, which in turn is overtly expressed to those around one.

Can we change our cynical beliefs about others? Will doing so make us less prone to anger and aggressive outbursts? And if so, will our risks of serious health problems be reduced?

The research I have described thus far suggests that the answer to the last question is yes. In part 2, I will describe some research suggesting the same for the first two questions. I will also provide some guidelines for assessing your own hostility level, and steps to reduce it if you find it too high.

But first there are two more kinds of evidence that should help convince you even more strongly of the harm hostility can do. The first concerns the very real biological pathways whereby hostility, particularly the anger that is fired by our cynical beliefs about the motives of others, sets in motion the chain of biological events that lead on to disease and death. The second body of evidence grows out of over two millennia of religious teachings that appear to lead to the same conclusion as the more "scientific" research described in the rest of this book. We also need to address the question, Where does hostility come from?

Before we move on to look at these areas, I want to conclude this chapter, filled as it has been with the unpleasant facts about hostility, on a more positive note.

THE TRUSTING HEART

As a physician, I have spent my professional life trying to understand better what is making people sick or killing them. But we also need to focus on trying to understand better what is making people healthier and keeping them alive into ripe old age.

There is, then, another message—the other side of the hostility coin—to be gleaned from the research results: Those who have a trusting heart are more likely to remain healthy throughout most of their lives and to live long.

What is the trusting heart?

The picture of the trusting heart that emerges from our research is, at its simplest definition, the opposite of that of the hostile heart.

The trusting heart believes in the basic goodness of humankind, that most people will be fair and kind in relationships with others. Having such beliefs, the trusting heart is slow to anger. Not seeking out evil in others, not expecting the worst of them, the trusting heart expects mainly good from others and, more often than not, finds it. As a result, the trusting heart spends little time feeling resentful, irritable, and angry.

From this it follows that the trusting heart treats others well, with consideration and kindness; the trusting heart almost never wishes or visits harm upon others.

Just as our research has shown that the hostile heart is at risk of premature death and disease, it also can reassure us that the trusting heart appears protected against these outcomes.

This is the other, more positive message of our research, and the best news of all.

FIVE

FROM MIND TO BODY: BIOLOGIC PATHWAYS FROM HOSTILITY TO DISEASE

Since the early 1980s, a research team at the Bowman-Gray School of Medicine in Winston-Salem, North Carolina, has been pursuing research to document whether psychological stress is capable of accelerating the formation of arteriosclerotic plaques, like the one that blocked John Smith's artery, in monkeys that are fed a high-fat diet (not unlike the fast-food fare that is a staple in the diet of many Americans).

To introduce stress into the lives of the monkeys they were studying, the researchers divided the monkeys, all males, into groups of five per cage. After about a month, the animals had established a pecking order within each cage, with one monkey dominant and the rest subservient to varying degrees. Three such groupings remained the same for the nearly one-year duration of this experiment and made up the low-stress group. An additional three groupings made up the stress group: at the end of each month they were shifted around, two monkeys from one group put into the same cage with three from another group, and so on. This resulted in renewed stress each month, as the animals battled to establish a new hierarchy.

When the monkeys' coronary arteries were examined at the completion of the study, the ones in the stress groups had more arteriosclerosis than those in the stable, low-stress groups. In the low-stress groups, the dominant monkeys had the least arteriosclerosis; but in the stress groups it was the dominant monkeys whose coronary arteries were the most riddled with blockages. The stress of the repeated social disruptions had led to more arteriosclerosis by itself; but with the extra stress the dominant monkeys had to face in order to maintain their position, the disease grew even worse.

This landmark study supplied the essential documentation we were looking for to show that psychosocial stress *does* affect biological processes involved in arteriosclerosis, and in so doing, justified efforts to identify the harmful biological processes in humans with high levels of hostility and anger.

The research showing that only those aspects of Type A behavior related to hostility are actually coronary-prone represents progress toward a better definition of coronary-prone behavior. In the process of identifying hostility—particularly cynicism, anger, and aggression—as the toxic part of Type A, we have also discovered that this same characteristic is a risk factor for a wide variety of other very serious illnesses. We have come this far with the aid of epidemiologic research approaches, simply documenting associations between hostility and disease in groups of patients and healthy persons.

This approach can take us only so far, however. The animal research I just described makes a good case that psychosocial stress has the potential to activate disease processes. But to understand how hostility leads to illness and death in humans, we must be able to identify those *biologic* characteristics of persons with high hostility levels that are the likely links between hostility, disease, and even death.

Why is it necessary to understand how hostility leads to disease? If we know hostility is the culprit, why not just do away with hostility and be done with the whole problem? Because not all components of hostility may be damaging, just as not all components of Type A behavior were found to be damaging. No purpose would be served in getting everybody to slow down, for example, if getting things done quickly is not a harmful trait unless driven by hostility. In fact, for people driven by a positive, enthusiastic approach to the world, getting things done quickly appears protective, and slowing them down could even be harmful. Similarly, if only those hostile individuals with certain biological characteristics are truly at risk, then incorporation of those biological characteristics into assessment procedures will identify those at high risk far more accurately than would assessment of hostility alone.

Most important, understanding the biologic pathways from hostility to disease will lead ultimately to the best preventive and treatment approaches. Epidemiologic approaches alone seldom provide sufficient information for complete solutions. They provide important clues as to the causes of disease in populations, but these must be complemented by biologic research if the most precise understanding of disease processes—and the most effective and efficient prevention and treatment—are to be achieved for the individual.

Consider, for example, the Black Death epidemic that was killing a large proportion of London's population in the mid-1600s. One of the first "epidemiologic" observations was that most of the deaths due to Plague occurred in the neighborhoods bordering the Thames River. This led to the conclusion that the cause of the disease was "evil vapours" rising from the river. Today we know that not "evil vapours" but the *Pasteurella pestis* bacteria, which is transmitted to humans when they are bitten by a louse that is carried on rats, was responsible for the Black Death, and why London's Great Fire of 1666 was "effective" in stopping its spread—it killed all the rats that harbored the lice that carried the *real* causative agent. Moving away from the Thames, which some Londoners tried, was never the solution to the problem, though all the observable evidence at the time pointed in that direction.

In short, epidemiology only provides us with clues as to where to look for the causative agent. Friedman and Rosenman's pioneering epidemiologic research identified a pattern of behaviors that was associated with increased coronary risk. Further epidemiologic research showed that only some aspects of this pattern, those concerned with hostility, are toxic. Now it is time to build upon these findings—to move on to identify biological pathways from hostility to disease.

While our knowledge of the biologic mechanisms accounting for the adverse effects of hostility on health is far less extensive at present than our knowledge of the epidemiologic associations of hostility, there are already emerging some promising leads regarding those bodily responses likely to be involved.

I'd like now to share with you a brief overview of some of the major systems the body uses to respond to stresses of various sorts, because I think it's helpful in understanding the biologic research we've done to date and the ramifications of our findings.

THE PHYSIOLOGY OF STRESS

The major body systems involved in adjustments to stress are illustrated, in simplified and schematic form, in Figure 5-1. Scientists and researchers argue endlessly over the best definition of "stress." For our purposes, it is simply any bit of sensory information that makes its way to the brain and leads to changes in the brain's communications to the body.

The brain uses three major communication systems to regulate bodily functions. The *voluntary nervous system* sends messages to the muscles so that we may respond appropriately to any given bit of sensory information, for example, when sight of a growling grizzly bear on a trail in Yellowstone Park prompts us to run as quickly as possible to the nearest tree and start climbing.

The second of the brain's communications systems is the *autonomic nervous system.* It's called "autonomic" because it works automatically, without our having to think about it. This system does its job via the combined actions

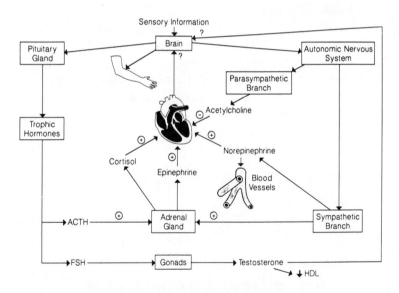

5-1. Schematic outline of body systems involved in responding to stress. See text for explanation of effects illustrated. As noted in the text, the parasympathetic branch is the "calming" branch, and the sympathetic branch of the autonomic nervous system is the "emergency" branch.

of its two branches, the "sympathetic," used mainly to get us going quickly in emergencies, and the "parasympathetic," whose function is mainly to keep the body's background maintenance systems—like digestion—in order and to calm the body's responses to the sympathetic branch. To help you keep the key functions of the two branches of the autonomic nervous system clearly in mind, throughout the rest of this book I shall use the term *emergency branch* to refer to the sympathetic branch, and *calming branch* for the parasympathetic branch. They have proven important to our work and bear closer scrutiny.

THE EMERGENCY BRANCH

The emergency branch helps the body respond to emergency situations—that grizzly bear again. This branch works via the actions of norepinephrine released from sympathetic nerves and epinephrine (familiar to most people as adrenaline) released from the adrenal gland.

Once released, norepinephrine and epinephrine act to stimulate two types of receptors—alpha and beta—in various tissues of the body. These receptors are like switches on the membranes of cells throughout the body. Once activated by the norepinephrine or epinephrine, the alpha or beta "switch" sets in motion a series of steps inside the cell. First, an enzyme, adenyl cyclase, is activated that converts adenosine triphosphate (ATP) to cyclic adenosine monophosphate (cyclic AMP). The cyclic AMP then goes on to activate other enzymes inside the cell, starting a cascade of events that leads to a variety of changes in that cell's functions, depending upon the type of cell being stimulated.

By initiating these steps, the emergency branch enables the body to respond quickly with the intense muscular efforts necessary to cope with stress. The heart, when prodded in this way by epinephrine and norepinephrine, works harder and increases the amount of blood it pumps from a resting value of about one gallon per minute to a peak value of about five gallons per minute.

Having two *different* sorts of receptors also enables the emergency branch to perform the useful task of regulating the distribution of the increased amount of blood being pumped by the heart among the various tissues and organs. Thus, stimulation by epinephrine of beta receptors in the arteries supplying blood to muscles causes these blood vessels to enlarge in order to deliver even more blood to the working muscles, supplying them with nutrients and oxygen and carrying away waste products. In contrast to the resting state, when only about 15 percent of the blood pumped by the heart is delivered to the muscular system, at peak exercise—climbing that tree with the grizzly right behind—over 80 percent of the blood being pumped by the heart is delivered to the muscles. This is due in part to the beta-receptor-stimulated enlargement of the muscle blood vessels.

The redistribution of blood pumped out by the heart is also helped by norepinephrine's stimulation of alpha receptors on blood vessels supplying the skin, the kidneys, and the digestive tract. While stimulation of blood vessel beta receptors causes the vessel to enlarge, stimulation of alpha receptors causes the vessels to contract, thereby reducing the flow of blood. Thus, the effect of the emergency branch's stimulation of the skin, kidney, and digestive-tract blood vessels is to reduce blood flow to these tissues, to shunt it away from them and to the working muscles. Not a bad idea, if you are being chased by a grizzly: If you are slashed by his claws, it is a good idea to shut down the blood flow to your skin. Besides, you can do without supplying the kidneys, gut, and skin for a while—right now, says your brain, all that extra blood is needed by those working muscles.

To better understand the purpose of all this activity,

it might help to think of the body as a large city in which, depending on the time of day and occurrences (e.g., a rock concert downtown or a fire in a suburb), there are wide swings in the traffic flow to various neighborhoods. Now imagine that this particular city's traffic department has a system that enables those in charge to change, simply by flipping a few switches, the width of all the roads in town. Thus, the roads in parts of town with sparse traffic could be immediately narrowed to only two lanes; and those where the traffic was especially heavy could just as quickly be widened to six, eight, even ten lanes. This kind of super-efficient trafficking system is just what our bodies have in the emergency branch of the autonomic nervous system.

In addition to the circulatory effects I've noted, the emergency branch also mobilizes fat stores from the fatty tissues and glucose from the liver. This capability provides for extra energy as needed during an emergency situation.

THE CALMING BRANCH

The other branch of the autonomic nervous system, the parasympathetic branch, is not usually thought to play a major role in responses to stress. Rather, it is believed to help maintain the body's "vegetative" functions. Since many of its actions appear to counter those of the sympathetic, or emergency, branch, it may help you to remember the major actions of the parasympathetic branch if you think of it as the "calming" branch—the branch that calms and soothes the body, thus preventing our remaining too long in a state of emergency mobilization, which, if left unchecked, could lead to disease.

Instead of norepinephrine and epinephrine, which stimulate alpha and beta adrenergic receptors, the calming branch, when activated—e.g., to counter emergency branch actions—releases another compound, acetylcholine, to stimulate the so-called muscarinic receptors. In a manner analogous to the use of cyclic AMP as the "second messenger" of the alpha and beta receptors of the emergency branch, stimulation of muscarinic receptors leads to formation inside the body's cells of cyclic GMP (guanosine monophosphate), the muscarinic second messenger, which in turn is responsible for events inside the cell that lead to calming-branch effects.

For example, when muscarinic receptors are activated, the digestive tract is stimulated to digest a meal, the heart rate slows down, the pupils of the eye become smaller, and the like. Of course these actions are generally not considered as part of the physiological response to stress, but, as we shall see later, some of the calming branch's actions do appear to be playing a key role in *blunting the harmful effects of the emergency branch's response to stress.*

Apart from the voluntary nervous system and the autonomic nervous system, the third major communication system available to the brain is the *neuroendocrine system,* which also acts automatically to maintain the body's internal milieu. This is illustrated in Figure 5-1, in which the brain's stimulation of the pituitary gland is shown to secrete certain "messenger" hormones into the blood. These hormones travel to distant "target glands," where they stimulate the glands to release other hormones, which, in turn, affect bodily processes, such as metabolic rate and sexual functions.

The major "stress hormone," apart from the epinephrine secreted by the adrenal gland, is cortisol, itself secreted—as shown in Figure 5-1—by a different part of the same adrenal gland. The precise steps whereby the brain causes the adrenal gland to secrete cortisol into the bloodstream are now known in exquisite detail, the result of an explosion of research in the field of neurobiology during the past decade.

The first step in this process is the release of CRF

(cortisol-releasing factor) from the hypothalamus, a collection of cells at the base of the brain that acts as a control center for the neuroendocrine system, where information regarding the outside world is sent from higher brain regions and from which appropriate action orders are issued to the body to enable it to meet the challenges implied by that information, or—equally important—by our *interpretation* of that information.

CRF is a peptide, a molecule made by collecting a series of amino acids together like pearls on a string. Once secreted by the hypothalamus, the CRF travels, via a small system of blood vessels, to the pituitary gland, where it stimulates the front part of that gland to release ACTH (adrenocorticotropic hormone) into the bloodstream. ACTH is another peptide hormone, which then travels in the blood to the adrenal gland, stimulating it to release cortisol into the blood.

At this point, cortisol becomes one of the "active ingredients" in the body's stress response. This hormone acts in a variety of ways to enhance and prolong the effects of the emergency branch of the autonomic nervous system. Cortisol stimulates the formation of both norepinephrine and epinephrine and inhibits their breakdown once released. Thus, cortisol makes more of these emergency branch "messengers" available to keep the emergency response going. Cortisol also acts to make both beta and alpha receptors more sensitive to norepinephrine and epinephrine. This would enable the necessary adjustments of bodily function to continue even after the emergency-branch messengers became depleted. These effects reflect cortisol's important role in maintaining the strength of the body's response in situations of *chronic* stress.

The brain will also prompt the pituitary gland to release another "messenger hormone," in this case FSH (follicle-stimulating hormone). This is another example of the neuroendocrine system in action. FSH travels via the bloodstream to the gonads, where it stimulates the release in men of the male sex hormone, testosterone.

The emergency-branch and cortisol responses appear to be called forth in situations that lead to the conclusion that "emergency measures" are needed, such as running from the growling grizzly bear. Testosterone responses, on the other hand, appear to occur under different circumstances: situations requiring vigilant observation of the environment.

Besides its involvement in sexual and aggressive behaviors, research in animals has also shown that testosterone improves the ability of the animal to focus and narrow its attention to some particular element in the environment, an effect that could improve performance in both sexual and aggressive pursuits. Once the organism perceives a threat to life or limb, however, testosterone secretion is actually suppressed, and the emergency-branch and cortisol responses take over.

THE PHYSIOLOGY OF HOSTILITY: CLUES FROM TYPE A STUDIES

Since we have just recently recognized that only the hostility aspects are toxic in Type A behavior, by far the bulk of the research done to date to identify biologic mechanisms linking coronary-prone behavior and coronary disease has focused mainly on differences in physiological responses between Type A and Type B men. Beginning with the first reports of increased risk of developing coronary disease in the Western Collaborative Group Study, researchers have been subjecting Type A and Type B men to various stressors to see if the Type As were more responsive physiologically. If they are, such larger responses could be the means whereby Type A (and hostility) is translated into disease.

As we shall see, this research is now being extended to include the biological correlates of hostility. The research on biological correlates of global Type A behavior is still important, however, since Type A still appears to place people at increased risk of developing *premature* coronary disease, that occurring prior to age 50. And by adding assessments of hostility to the Type A assessments in these studies, it has been possible to begin clarifying the biological correlates of hostility.

To provide realistic stressors, researchers have resorted to many ingenious strategies. In one important early study, Friedman and Rosenman had Type A and Type B men come into a room and sit on either side of a table, in the middle of which had been placed a bottle of very expensive French wine. In front of each man was placed a sort of jigsaw puzzle, the pieces all mixed up. They were told that whoever could put his puzzle together first would win the bottle of wine. As the men began working, loud rock music started to blast from concealed speakers in the room. This went on for several minutes, until the men were told to stop. No one ever finished the puzzle because there really was no solution.

Blood samples were drawn from the participants in this study at the start and after they were told to stop trying to solve the puzzle. The samples were later analyzed to determine the amount of norepinephrine and epinephrine that had been released into the blood by the emergency branch of the autonomic nervous system. At the start of the experiment, the Type A and B men had similar levels of these compounds. At the end, however, after they had been trying to win the bottle of wine, the norepinephrine levels were far higher in the Type A men.

A similar study was conducted by Dr. David Glass in New York City, using firemen and policemen as subjects who were asked to play a Pong computer game. Instead of competing against each other, the Type A and B men in this study competed against a man who was presented as another fireman or policeman, but who, in reality, was an accomplice of Dr. Glass and an expert Pong player. Not only did he always beat the other players in the game, but he also harassed them with disparaging remarks about their ability to play the game, their clumsiness, even their manhood.

Again, blood samples were obtained and analyzed for epinephrine and norepinephrine. Epinephrine levels were higher among the Type A men after the game was finished.

About the time these studies were conducted, Dr. Dembroski was carrying out an extensive series of investigations in which he evaluated blood-pressure and heart-rate responses of Type A and B subjects when challenged to do their best in playing computer games. The first researcher to report increased blood-pressure and heart-rate reactivity among Type A subjects, Dr. Dembroski not surprisingly was also the first to find as a result of this study that subjects rated high on Potential for Hostility showed larger responses when they were aggressively challenged to perform various tasks in the laboratory.

In addition to larger increases in blood epinephrine and norepinephrine levels and larger increases in blood pressure and heart rate, Type As have been found to show greater changes in their electrocardiogram (EKG) that are also consistent with more pronounced emergency-branch responses to stress. Figure 5-2 shows a typical EKG complex made up of several waves, labeled P, Q, R, S, and T. These waves represent the electrical manifestations of the action of the heart. The P wave is generated by the contraction of the two atria—small chambers that receive the blood returning from the body and lungs and pump it into the right and left ventricles, respectively, from which the blood is pumped back to the lungs or the other parts of the

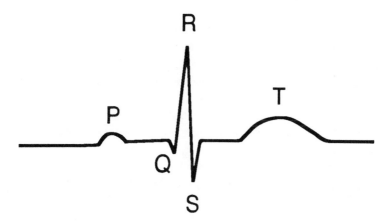

5-2. Drawing of a typical electrocardiographic tracing showing the various waves that reflect the electrical activity of the heart during a single cycle's beat. See text for explanation.

body. The QRS complex represents the spread of electrical activity through the two ventricles as they contract to pump blood throughout the body. Finally, the T wave reflects the electrical recovery—"repolarization"—of the ventricular muscle cells, a process that is necessary in order to ready them to respond to the next wave of electrical signals with another pumping contraction. Basic research into the factors that influence the heart's electrical activity as reflected in the EKG has shown that increased emergency-branch stimulation of the heart will cause a reduction in the height of the T wave.

For this reason, researchers Lawrence Van Egeren and John Furedy have used such stressors as competitive games and mental-arithmetic tasks to study the effects upon the EKG T wave in Type A and B subjects. Consistent with the research looking at other emergency-branch effects, they found that the T-wave height decreased more during stress among Type A men than it did among Type Bs. They interpreted this greater T-wave attenuation among the Type As as reflecting a larger emergency-branch impact on the heart of Type As.

Taken altogether, these studies provide consistent evidence that, whatever the stimulus employed, when the fight-or-flight response is activated in the laboratory, the Type As show more pronounced responses of the emergency branch of the autonomic nervous system, whether one uses blood pressure and heart rate, blood levels of epinephrine and norepinephrine, or the height of the T wave on the EKG to assess emergency-branch reactivity. Such excessive responses could be damaging to the heart and arteries, especially if repeated frequently over a long span of time.

Although, as described in chapters 3 and 4, my major research interest during the mid-to-late 1970s focused on trying to identify those psychological traits that are the coronary-prone aspects of Type A behavior, I always had a strong interest in understanding their underlying biological pathways. My first research project, completed in medical school twenty-five years ago, addressed the question of how bodily responses to stress might play a role in causing disease. With encouragement and guidance from Dr. Pat McKegney, I spent one summer wheeling around from ward to ward a large, cumbersome machine that was able to measure blood pressure automatically while I interviewed every Yale Hospital patient with high blood pressure I could find.

I learned that blood pressure increased when patients were involved in an interview in which their illness, their family life, and other personal topics were brought up in an engaging way by the interviewer. Compared to patients suffering from other illnesses, those with high blood pressure showed larger and more prolonged blood-pressure increases during the interview—thus exposing their blood vessels and heart to further damage.

After I went to the National Institute of Mental

Health (NIMH) in 1970 for a two-year tour of duty, I continued my work on the physiology of stress. More important, I learned about a far broader range of research techniques for studying stress responses, including the measurement of a wide array of stress hormones and the measurement of muscle blood flow—an important component of the fight-or-flight response.

I was able to make a modest contribution to our knowledge of the physiology of stress during those years at NIMH by demonstrating that, apart from the increase in muscle blood flow during fight-or-flight situations, there is an opposite response, a constriction of muscle blood vessels, when vigilant observation of environmental stimuli is required. (This had already been observed in animal responses.) This led me to believe it was important to study not only the fight-or-flight response but also the vigilance response in trying to identify biologic characteristics of Type As that might lead to coronary disease. It also struck me as important to study other hormones besides those associated with the emergency branch's contribution to stress responses—especially the neuroendocrine branch's major stress hormone, cortisol.

After I came to Duke, my first study on biologic mechanisms of coronary-prone behavior focused on young Type A and B male undergraduates who came to my laboratory for two sessions, one week apart. During one session they performed a mental-arithmetic task (serial subtractions of 13 from a large number), with a prize offered to the student who performed the most subtractions. During the other, they performed a vigilance task—watching signals on a TV screen and pushing a button whenever a specified pattern of letters appeared. In rest periods before and during the task, we measured blood pressure, heart rate, and muscle blood flow at one-minute intervals. A needle had been placed in one of the arm veins an hour before the experiment started, and this was used during the rest and task periods to obtain blood samples that we later assayed for various hormones that might be responsive to the stressors.

The results of this study, published in the journal *Science* in 1982, are shown in Table 5-1. When performing mental arithmetic problems for a prize, the Type A men increased their muscle blood flow more and showed larger increases in blood levels of norepinephrine, epinephrine, and cortisol. Testosterone levels did not change in response to mental arithmetic. In marked contrast, all of the responses that were larger for Type As during the mental arithmetic task did not show large increases during the vigilance task, nor were the As and Bs different. What did

Table 5-1.   Differing biological responses of young Type A and Type B men to mental arithmetic and vigilance tasks. (Adapted from data in *Science*, 1982, vol. 218, pp. 483–85.

	TYPE A MEN	TYPE B MEN
Responses to Mental Arithmetic		
Muscle blood flow	+ + + +	+ +
Norepinephrine	+ + + +	+ +
Epinephrine	+ + + +	±
Cortisol	+ + + +	±
Testosterone	±	±
Responses to Vigilance		
Muscle blood flow	±	±
Norepinephrine	+ +	+ +
Epinephrine	±	±
Cortisol	±	±
Testosterone	+ + +	±

differentiate the As and Bs during vigilance behavior was testosterone: the Type A men showed larger increases.

This study confirmed several important points from earlier studies: that Type A men showed larger emergency-branch responses when the fight-or-flight response is stimulated; that a newly identified stress hormone, cortisol, is more responsive among Type As; and that during vigilance task performance, Type A men show a larger testosterone response than Type Bs.

But what about hostility? Even though the study just described was done before we were sure that hostility was the only toxic part of Type A, are there any clues in the results that shed light on how the biological characteristics of hostile persons may be harmful? When we evaluated the responses to the mental-arithmetic task, no differences appeared between subjects with high versus low scores on the Ho scale. Ho scores did add, however, to Type A in identifying those young men with larger versus smaller testosterone responses to the vigilance task. The largest testosterone increases were found in the Type As who also had high Ho scores, while the smallest responses (decreases, actually) were found in Type Bs with low Ho scores.

Thus, Ho levels did not relate to biological responses to a competitive game like mental arithmetic, but were associated with blood testosterone responses to a vigilance task. This makes some sense, in that there is no readily evident reason why the psychological characteristics of the person with high Ho scores—cynical mistrust, anger, and aggression—should be stimulated more by the demands of performing mental arithmetic for a prize. (The other aspects of the Type A person, time urgency and desire to achieve, would be expected to lead to larger responses during such a task.)

On the other hand, a mistrusting individual might be expected to be more vigilant in many situations: since he does not trust others, he must be ever observant to make sure they are not doing something wrong. Indeed, as we learned earlier, testosterone has been shown in animal studies to facilitate the focusing and narrowing of attention that occurs with vigilance. This effect, coupled with the effects of testosterone to increase aggressive and dominance behaviors, makes the high Ho subjects' increased testosterone response during the vigilance task all the more understandable. On a more speculative note, and as we shall consider in more detail later on when we consider the origins of hostility, it is possible that increased testosterone responses could be a biological *cause* of high hostility levels.

For the present, let us note that all of these larger responses in Type As are quite plausibly playing a role in increased coronary risk, particularly, as the research cited earlier suggests, coronary disease that becomes manifest before age 50: Norepinephrine, epinephrine, and cortisol all have effects upon the cardiovascular system that could greatly increase the risk of suffering acute coronary events, like the ones that afflicted Mary Smith and John Smith.

The effects of these hormones could also be important contributors to the premature development of coronary arteriosclerosis. We still do not have a complete understanding of all those steps whereby arteriosclerotic blockages (known as "plaques") form and grow in arteries. The most widely accepted theory currently is that the process starts with some injury to the inner lining (known as the endothelium) of the artery. If blood cholesterol levels are high, the cholesterol begins to accumulate at the injury site. Blood platelets are attracted to that spot and release chemicals that stimulate the growth of the muscular wall of the artery.

Among the factors that have been described as possible injurers of the endothelium are: increased blood pressure; turbulent blood flow around arterial branching points; chemicals (for example, high cholesterol itself); even viral infections. Since stress hormones can contribute to all these factors, it is clear that large and frequent increases in the emergency- and neuroendocrine-branch components of the stress response, as have been found in Type As, are likely contributors to endothelial injury.

Beyond this sort of circumstantial evidence, patients with Cushing's disease, which is characterized by high blood cortisol levels, have long been known to suffer a very high rate of arteriosclerotic complications. And in studies of animals fed a high-fat diet to increase arteriosclerosis, administration of excess cortisol has been found to increase the rate of arteriosclerotic plaque formation.

The larger testosterone responses of the more hostile Type As during vigilance behaviors could also be part of the story. You will recall that not all components of the blood cholesterol level are bad, that the HDL fraction is actually protective against risk of coronary disease. While women have higher HDL levels than men, a difference that has been proposed as at least part of the explanation for lower coronary risk among women, this difference does not become evident until after puberty. Before puberty, boys' and girls' HDL levels are the same; after puberty, but after the boys' testosterone levels have risen, the HDL levels come down. As with cortisol, administration of extra testosterone has been found to increase arteriosclerosis in animal experiments.

The Bowman-Gray research with monkeys cited earlier certainly shows that in animals closely related to humans, frequent arousals of the fight-or-flight response *can* lead to more severe arteriosclerosis.

Just as with Type A and, more recently, hostility, the acid test of whether these biological characteristics are actually involved will depend upon the results of prospective studies that ask: do those with larger responses of the sorts described above show *increased subsequent risk* of developing coronary heart disease? Meanwhile, we are left with a high level of suspicion that such biological responses are very likely the links between Type A behavior (and probably hostility, too) and coronary risk.

For those of us who are convinced that *something* about Type A behavior is bad for the heart, it is reassuring to find that there is very good evidence that the excessive hormonal responses we have seen among Type As in lab situations generalize to the real world. To evaluate hormonal functions in persons going about their daily activities, researchers ask them to save their urine over a twenty-four-hour period. Since all of the hormones in which we are interested as a result of the lab studies—norepinephrine, epinephrine, cortisol, and testosterone—are excreted in the urine, it is possible by measuring them in urine samples taken over the course of a day to obtain a good indication of how much of each hormone the person actually secretes during that period.

In an early study of some of the men in the Western Collaborative Group Study, Friedman and Rosenman found that the Type As excreted more testosterone in their urine during the working hours, but not during the night-time hours. In a study just completed at Duke, we found that middle-aged Type A men also excrete more epinephrine and norepinephrine across the twenty-four-hour period when compared to the Type B men. Thus, excessive hormonal responses among Type As are not confined to the lab setting, but are also to be found in more "real life" situations.

A PROTECTIVE ROLE
FOR THE CALMING BRANCH?

Another, quite different approach to the task of identifying biological mechanisms of coronary-prone behavior was suggested by a young Japanese physician, Dr. Hirokazu Monou, who was doing a fellowship with me in the early 1980s while he was on leave from Tohoku University Medical School's Department of Psychosomatic Medicine in Sendai, Japan.

Since we had already found, as had several other research groups, that Type As show larger epinephrine responses to laboratory stressors, he reasoned that emergency-branch beta receptors might be "down-regulated" in Type As as compared to Type Bs. Down-regulation of receptors occurs when a receptor is exposed over long periods to high levels of the messenger chemical that stimulates it. The process of down-regulation serves the useful purpose of protecting the body from excessive, potentially harmful effects of prolonged physiological activation. (It also explains why your nose spray stops working to unplug your stuffy nose after a certain number of applications.)

Since it appeared that Type As respond with excessive epinephrine secretion in both the lab and real life, Dr. Monou reasoned that their beta receptors should be down-regulated. To test this hypothesis, he proposed that we use intravenous infusions of isoproterenol (a synthetic form of epinephrine) to stimulate the beta receptors of Type A and B subjects. (Unlike epinephrine, which stimulates beta receptors more, but also has some effect on alpha receptors, isoproterenol stimulates only beta receptors.) If the high levels of epinephrine release were occurring more on a daily basis in the Type As, their beta-receptor-mediated physiological responses to the isoproterenol infusions should be smaller than those of the Type Bs.

I thought Dr. Monou's hypothesis to be sound. If the Type As did indeed show smaller beta-receptor-mediated responses, it would be exciting evidence that they are actually secreting more epinephrine day in and day out and that could explain the damaging element at work in Type As. There was another appealing feature of the approach he suggested: It bypassed the issue of "cognitive mediation" of differences between individuals in responses to behavioral stressors. When Type As and Bs are given various laboratory tasks to perform, such as mental arithmetic, video games, and the like, it is hard to be sure what is responsible for the differences observed in their physiological responses. Perhaps the Type As were not as smart as the Bs and this is why the arithmetic was "more stressful" for them, or perhaps they had poorer hand-eye coordination that made the video game harder for them. It was hard, if not impossible, to really know which of the differences in what goes on in the "black box" that lies between doing the task and the biological responses—i.e., the brain—were responsible for the response differences.

Giving intravenous infusions of isoproterenol, on the other hand, bypassed the black box. We could be precise in giving the same dose of drug—so many micrograms per kilogram per minute—to each subject, and in having considerable confidence that any differences in his physiological responses to the drug were mainly that, physiological and not psychologically mediated. Thus, taking this pharmacological approach should enable us to see if there are basic *biological* differences between Type As and Type Bs.

In fact, we did find basic biological differences, though not the ones we had expected. First of all, the isoproterenol infusions had exactly the desired effects: with a low-dose infusion, the heart rate and muscle blood flow increased a moderate amount; and with infusion of a higher dose, these beta-receptor-mediated responses increased even more. As you will recall, when the beta receptor is activated, its physiological effects result from the actions of increased formation within the cell of its "second messenger," cyclic AMP. Blood samples obtained before and after the isopreterenol infusions were analyzed for cyclic AMP levels, therefore, and these also showed clear increases after the infusions. So far, so good—the isoproterenol infusions were having exactly the predicted effects on beta receptor–mediated functions.

But when we compared these responses—heart rate, muscle blood flow, and blood levels of cyclic AMP—in the Type A and Type B subjects of this study, there were no differences. Type As and Bs were virtually identical in their response to the isoproterenol infusion. We had not been successful in proving the hypothesis that Type As would be *less* responsive to isoproterenol infusions due to down-regulation of their beta receptors. A disappointment, but hardly the first time a good idea has not panned out.

In considering whether a surgeon is properly evaluating patients with possible appendicitis, hospital review boards begin to worry that the surgeon is not operating on all the patients he or she should be taking to surgery if a significant proportion of the removed appendixes do not come back from pathology with a reading of "normal appendix." In other words, the surgeon who does not remove some normal appendixes is felt to have too high a threshold for taking patients to the operating room—a situation that, eventually, will cause some patients who should have their appendixes removed to go without surgery for too long.

Similarly, a researcher who does not have some "misses" in the studies he or she does is probably not pursuing enough of the good ideas that come along. An equally important reason not to be too cautious in pursuing research ideas is that often, even though the main idea does not work out, the research uncovers some new findings that ultimately prove to be even more exciting than those based on the original hypothesis guiding a given experiment. Dr. Fleming did not set out to discover penicillin, nor was Roentgen planning to discover X rays when he had photographic plates in the same room as the cathode ray tube he was using in his experiments. Yet those discoveries turned out ultimately to be far more important than the original hypotheses being tested by either man.

So it was that, while we did not have much success in proving our hypothesis that beta receptors should be down-regulated in Type As, through sheer accident we did discover something entirely unforeseen—something that I believe will ultimately prove to be far more important.

Let me set the scene. Although isoproterenol is a very safe drug to administer in healthy persons (and even most sick individuals) it is not without some risk, mainly having to do with increased likelihood of heart rhythm abnormalities, for example, premature ventricular contractions like those that worried Mary Smith's doctors early in her illness. To protect our subjects against even the small risk of such complications of isoproterenol administration, it was necessary to have a physician monitor their EKG throughout the experiment, so that any heart rhythm problems could be noted and appropriate protective measures taken immediately.

That was my job in this study. Dr. Monou and Nan McCown, the research nurse who has been involved in our research program for several years, were in the room with the young Type A and B men who volunteered to be subjects in this study. They inserted the needle in the arm vein and carefully monitored the subjects during the administration of the high and low doses of isoproterenol. They also were ready to administer drugs needed to counter any rhythm abnormalities that might develop. It was my task to sit in the adjacent room containing the equipment used to monitor the cardiovascular functions of the subjects during the experiment and watch the EKG as it was written out on the polygraph—watch it very closely, to make sure that no abnormal rhythms were occurring and, if so, to alert Nan and Hiro immediately.

For the first couple of subjects everything went smoothly, so smoothly that it quickly became somewhat boring to sit there and watch the EKG for nearly an hour, from baseline periods through isoproterenol infusions, through recovery periods. Nevertheless, watch it I did, for it was important to detect immediately any heart rhythm

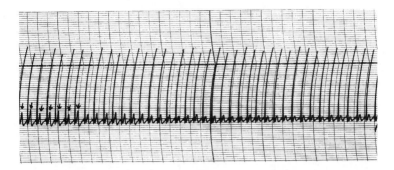

5-3. Actual EKG tracing from one of the men in our isoproterenol infusion study. The isoproterenol infusion had started about one minute before the start of the tracing that is shown. The T waves, marked by arrows in the first few beats, decrease in height during the approximately 50 seconds of this tracing.

disturbances, so that the infusion could be stopped. During the isoproterenol infusion on the day we were running the third subject, I suddenly became aware, as I sat there staring at the EKG, that something was happening that I had not anticipated.

What I saw is illustrated in Figure 5-3. The taller upright waves are the R waves, electrical reflections of the heart muscle's contraction to pump blood around the body. Just after the R waves come the T waves, the first few marked in Figure 5-3 by arrows. You will recall that T waves reflect recovery of heart muscle, to be ready to contract again. As I watched the polygraph paper move along under the EKG pen, I suddenly realized that the T waves were *decreasing* in height before my eyes.

We went back and saw that the height of the first subject's T waves had also decreased during the isoproterenol infusion, though perhaps not as dramatically as those of the subject whose T waves first caught my attention. From then on, we closely watched the T waves during each infusion study. We were not disappointed. Sooner or later during the infusion, in nearly every subject we studied, the

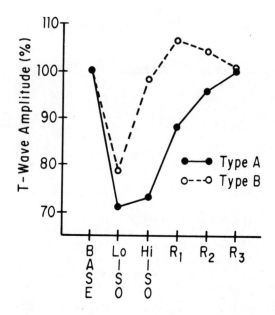

5-4.   Differing response of T-wave height (amplitude) in young Type A and Type B men to intravenous isoproterenol infusions. See text for explanation. (Reprinted with permission from *Health Psychology*, 1988, in press.)

T waves would begin to shorten, much the same as those shown in Figure 5-3.

By the time this study was about one-third finished, Dr. Monou had returned to Japan, and his place had been taken by another young member of the Department of Psychosomatic Medicine at Tohoku University Medical School, Dr. Motoyazu Muranaka. With Moto's able involvement we continued the study until we had run ten Type As and ten Type Bs through the isoproterenol-infusion protocol. With meticulous care, Moto used calipers to measure accurately the height of the T waves in each infusion study.

The result is shown in Figure 5-4. During the low-dose isoproterenol infusion, the T waves of both Type A and B subjects showed a similar decrease in height, about 25 percent. When the infusion rate was doubled, however, the two groups diverged. The T waves stayed down in the Type A subjects and only slowly recovered over the three five-minute recovery periods. Among the Type Bs, the picture was remarkably different: Even during the high-dose infusion, the height of their T waves had fully recovered to baseline levels. Statistical analysis showed that, unlike the other beta-receptor-mediated responses, these T-wave responses were very reliably different in the Type As and Bs.

Even though both were receiving the same dose for their weights, the Type As were showing a more prolonged decrease in the height of their T waves as the isoproterenol infusion continued. In trying to understand what was going on here, we immediately thought of the studies by other researchers, in which stress led to larger decreases in T-wave height among the Type A subjects. But these differences were felt to represent greater emergency-branch responses in the Type As, as noted earlier. In our infusion study, there was no reason to expect any difference in the amount of emergency-branch stimulation of the heart—all subjects received equal intravenously administered doses. And we had objective evidence, in the form of the equal heart rate, muscle blood flow, and cyclic AMP responses, that our Type A and B subjects were showing equal responses to their equipotent isoproterenol doses. It was clear that *something else was at work here*, something other than a larger emergency-branch response among the Type As.

I was at a loss for a viable alternative explanation. In such circumstances it is always a good policy to seek advice from wiser heads. The first person I went to was my colleague in Duke's Department of Pharmacology, Dr. Saul Schanberg. Saul has been a good adviser and coworker on my neuroendocrine research ever since I arrived at Duke in 1972. Saul was also at a loss to explain the T-wave results.

But, as usual, he didn't let me down—he did offer some advice that proved useful: "If anybody can figure this stuff out, it's Maddie Spach."

Dr. Madison Spach is a professor of pediatrics at Duke specializing in pediatric cardiology. He has pioneered the development of sophisticated techniques for studying the spread of electrical activity across the heart muscle and is one of the top pediatric cardiology researchers in the U.S. Although he also scratched his head at first when we showed him the tracings of the T waves becoming smaller and smaller as the isoproterenol infusions continued, Maddie slowly began to nod his head saying, "You know, this could be parasympathetic antagonism." (You will recall this refers to what earlier we termed the "calming" branch of the autonomic nervous system.) He gave us some references to look up and wished us good luck in figuring out what we were dealing with.

Although he spoke excellent English, Dr. Muranaka always made notes in the margins of journal articles in Japanese script. Moto soon began to fill my "in" box with copies of the papers Maddie Spach had suggested, as well as many more that were cited in those papers. I could gauge Moto's assessment of each paper by the volume of Japanese writing in the margins.

Those papers with the most Japanese annotations dealt with the phenomenon of the calming (parasympathetic) branch's antagonism of the activity and actions of the emergency branch of the autonomic nervous system. I described earlier how the calming branch stimulates various vegetative functions (such as digesting a meal) via the effects of acetylcholine on muscarinic receptors.

In addition to these "body maintenance" functions, the calming branch's muscarinic receptors serve another function—to retard or inhibit the actions of the emergency branch. The basic biology of how this is accomplished has been worked out in some detail. For our purposes, what is important to understand is that the calming branch can effectively "turn off" the heart's responses to emergency-branch stimulation.

Returning now to the different T-wave responses to isoproterenol in our young Type A and B men, since other beta receptor responses were identical, we began to suspect that the better T-wave recovery in the Bs might well be the result of a more robust calming branch's antagonism of the isoproterenol effects to reduce the height of their T waves. Instead of the conclusion drawn from studies using psychological stressors (that Type As show larger emergency branch responses), by using this drug approach to generate equal levels of emergency-branch stimulation of the heart, we may have uncovered an entirely different sort of mechanism accounting for A-B differences: *a more robust calming-branch antagonism of the emergency-branch effects among Type Bs.*

We sought additional evidence of stronger calming-branch responses among the Type Bs, and got it, from another study we conducted shortly after the isoproterenol study.

Most mammals, especially ones like seals and otters but also humans, are able to dive beneath the surface of water and remain there for long periods through the activation of the "dive reflex." A hallmark of this reflex is a marked slowing of the heart rate, sponsored by the calming branch's input. Thus, by stimulating the dive reflex, we knew we could assess the strength of the calming branch's response to a standard stimulus.

We can stimulate the dive reflex in humans by having them immerse their face in ice water. The same effect can be achieved by simply placing a plastic bag filled with a mixture of ice and water over the forehead, which achieves the same ends without requiring the subjects to hold their breath. We followed the latter approach in our next study of another group of healthy young Type A and B men, ten of each.

The results of this study confirmed our expectation that the Type Bs would show more prolonged calming-branch responses; in this case, slowing of the heart rate. As shown in Figure 5-5, both As and Bs had exactly the same heart rate prior to our placing the ice bag on their foreheads. After one minute, both had shown identical decreases in heart rate. After two minutes, however, their heart rates had diverged in dramatic fashion: The Type Bs' heart rate had slowed even more, indicating continuing calming-branch input to the heart; but the Type As' heart rate had speeded back to the baseline level, indicating a waning of the calming-branch input to their hearts.

Here, then, was another form of evidence, complementing our T-wave findings, that suggests Type Bs are distinguished from Type As not only by *smaller* emergency-branch and hormonal responses to stress, but also by

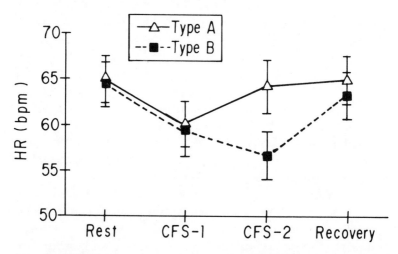

5-5. Differing heart-rate responses of Type A and B men to application of an ice pack to the forehead: there are no heart-rate differences at rest and after one minute (CFS-1), but after two minutes (CFS-2) the heart rates have diverged. (Reprinted with permission from *Psychophysiology*, 1988, vol. 25, p. 335.)

larger calming-branch responses that actually attenuate the effects of emergency-branch activation. Just as the larger emergency-branch responses of Type As can stimulate processes of arterial injury leading to arteriosclerosis and heart attacks, the stronger calming-branch responses of Type Bs could serve to protect them by turning off the harmful actions of the emergency branch on their heart and blood vessels before damage is done.

You may be asking, this is fine for Type A and B, but what about hostility, the toxic part? As I said at the outset, there is more evidence regarding the biologic aspects of Type A behavior simply because Type A has been known and studied as a coronary risk factor longer, our appreciation of the central role hostility plays coming only recently. Even though we still focused on the A-B comparisons in these biologic studies, it has been possible to use the results to evaluate potential effects of hostility.

Just as Ho scores contributed to a better prediction of testosterone responses to the vigilance task in an earlier study, we questioned whether Ho scores would also improve our ability to see a stronger calming-branch effect on T-wave responses to isoproterenol infusions. They did. All ten Type A subjects in the infusion study had very poor recovery of T-wave height during the high-dose isoproterenol infusion. In contrast, of the ten Type B subjects, six showed good recovery of T-wave height during the high-dose infusion. Of the four Type Bs with poor T-wave recovery, in the same low range as all ten Type As, three had *high* Ho scores, and the fourth had a positive family history of early coronary disease.

Thus, Ho scores combined with Type A-B assessments led to better prediction of both T-wave responses to isoproterenol and testosterone response to vigilance tasks. This evidence encouraged us to conclude that hostility levels, as assessed by the Ho scale, were associated with biologic response characteristics likely to place high Ho scorers at higher disease risk.

THE PHYSIOLOGY OF
HOSTILITY: SUCCESS AT LAST

I continued to be disappointed, however, by our inability to find any Ho effects in the responses to mental arithmetic. Mental arithmetic clearly was a good stimulus for the fight-or-flight response, causing as it did very reliable increases in muscle blood flow, not to mention increases in stress hormones, at least in Type A subjects. Although the relationship of Ho scores to testosterone and T-wave responses helped identify potential biologic mechanisms responsible for the toxic effects of hostility, it would make our case even stronger if the size of fight-or-flight responses was also predicted by hostility. Use of the mental-arithmetic approach was not helping to achieve that goal, neither in our hands nor in the hands of others who were beginning to publish papers on the same subject.

As I noted earlier, while it seemed reasonable to expect that hostility would predict increased vigilance, and, hence, increased testosterone levels during vigilance behavior, there was no similarly obvious reason why hostility should influence the biological correlates of mental-arithmetic task performance. More reasonable, it seemed to me, would be some task in which the hostile person's suspiciousness and mistrust of others was activated, leading to more anger, which should, in turn, generate a concomitant increase in fight-or-flight responding.

In an early study we tried to harass subjects doing mental-arithmetic tasks by having an assistant come in after a few minutes and tell them to stop moving their arms because it was interfering with the measurements. After another few minutes, the assistant returned and, in a harsher and more combative tone, warned the subjects that they were really "messing up the measurements and had better stay still for the last few minutes of the experiment, or we'll have to throw out all your data."

This study was partially successful, in that the subjects with high Ho scores rated their anger as being higher than did the low Ho scoring subjects. In addition, the higher the anger following the second harassment, the larger was the increase in muscle blood flow. But, try as we might, we were unable to show a direct relationship between Ho scores and any of the biologic responses to the mental arithmetic, even with harassment.

It was not until very recently—in a study that was the brainchild of Dr. Edward Suarez, a young psychologist doing a postdoctoral fellowship with me—that we have been successful in clearly showing the expected relationship between high Ho scores and more pronounced emergency-branch responses during a fight-or-flight situation.

As part of his postdoctoral training Ed had learned about physiological monitoring techniques and familiarized himself with our earlier, only partially successful efforts to find biological correlates of high Ho scores. He soon became convinced that our earlier approaches had not adequately tapped into the hostility characteristics of our subjects. This was obvious for mental arithmetic, but even our harassment procedure had been, Ed felt, not as realistic as necessary.

Ed proceeded to devise a harassment procedure that he felt would tap into the hostility of high Ho scoring subjects. This procedure led our subjects to believe their performance on a lab task was being unfairly criticized, mimicking real-life situations we have all experienced at one time or another. Ed's strategy fulfilled our highest expectations. When performing the task without harassment, subjects with high and low Ho scores showed *similar* increases in blood pressure and muscle blood flow, confirming the earlier findings that Ho scores do not predict biologic responses to simple mental tasks. When harassment was added, however, the high and low Ho subjects' responses diverged dramatically. In contrast to all the other groups, the harassed high-scoring Ho subjects showed *larger* increases in muscle blood flow and blood pressure during the task and even showed much slower recovery in these functions following the task.

An additional finding was that, when we later had the subjects rate how angry they felt during the experiment, both high and low Ho subjects reported more anger when harassed. But blood pressure, heart rate, and muscle blood flow increased with increasing anger ratings *only* for the high Ho subjects. The low Ho subjects' anger increased, but their biological responses were not linked—unlike those of the high Ho subjects—to the anger aroused by Ed's harassment. Apparently, *anger has a real biological cost, but only for subjects with high hostility.* If you are a hostile person, learning to reduce or avoid anger could be an important strategy to avoid these biological costs.

Suarez's study solved a lot of our earlier problems. By providing a more realistic situation that taps into the high Ho scorer's psychological characteristics, Ed had demonstrated biologic consequences of having those characteristics that could lead to disease.

The research on biological pathways is not complete. We are now carrying out further studies to examine the hormonal correlates of Ho scores using Ed's experimental approach. Further drug studies will be done to understand better the protective role of the calming (parasympathetic) branch among nonhostile Type B subjects. I am confident this further research will take us closer to the ultimate goal of not only understanding the biologic pathways from hostility to disease, but also being able to interdict those pathways and thereby reduce the disease toll exacted by hostility.

Meanwhile, it's becoming increasingly clear that when stressed, particularly in ways that activate their mistrust of others and thus generate anger, more hostile individuals show enhanced activation of emergency (sympathetic) branch and hormonal responses that make up the fight-or-flight response. If experienced more frequently and more intensively day in and day out, such responses could very definitely contribute to increased disease risk.

When stimulated to be especially vigilant, more hostile individuals secrete more of the male sex hormone testosterone. This, also, could contribute to disease processes, particularly arteriosclerosis, via effects to lower levels of the "good" cholesterol, HDL.

Coming at the disease process from an entirely different direction—from the perspective of protective, rather than harmful, biologic mechanisms—there is growing evidence that persons low in hostility may be protected from the ravages of their emergency-branch responses by the more robust "braking" action of the calming (parasympathetic) branch of their autonomic nervous system.

Thus, in addition to the large body of epidemiologic evidence implicating hostility as a serious threat to health, there is a growing amount of research that is helping to identify the biological mechanisms responsible for the harm done by hostility.

Where, you may be wondering at this point, does hostility come from? Do we have to learn to be hostile, or are the origins of hostility bred in our genes, perhaps along with the biological characteristics described in this chapter? And is all this knowledge new, or can we find forewarnings in the past?

To find out, read on.

SIX

THE ORIGINS OF HOSTILITY: NATURE AND/OR NURTURE

R esearch into the connections between behavior and disease has identified hostility as a key psychological aspect of the individual's makeup that predisposes to coronary heart disease, as well as a wide variety of other death-causing maladies. Within the domain of hostility, certain aspects appear more important than others in leading to serious illness. These include cynicism, or a basic mistrust of the motives and intentions of others; a more frequent and intense experience of anger; and the tendency to express such angry feelings in overtly aggressive behavior.

We have also learned that more hostile persons show biological responses under certain conditions that might account for their early development of serious disease. When angered by interpersonal confrontations, the more hostile persons show more pronounced cardiovascular responses characteristic of the fight-or-flight response. Under conditions requiring vigilant observation of the environment, they secrete more testosterone. Less hostile individuals, on the other hand, appear to have a more robust calming branch of their autonomic nervous system, resulting in a more rapid arrest of emergency-branch activation.

These conclusions in hand, our next task is to determine how these characteristics come to exist in the individual in the first place. What are the origins of hostility? Why are some persons more trusting than others? Why do some people produce larger biological responses than others during arguments or when vigilant? Why does the calming branch of others intercede to halt the emergency-branch activity? Do some people have larger biological responses because they are hostile; or are they hostile because of their larger biological responses? Is hostility learned during the course of growing up; or are we born with the template of hostility in our genes? Answers to these questions will lead eventually to a better understanding of how to prevent the development of hostility in the first place, before it has become entrenched, and before the biological processes that lead to disease have been set in motion.

During the same decades in which Friedman and Rosenman were formulating and testing the Type A hypothesis and while that hypothesis was being refined, psychologists interested in human development focused their attention on the development of important human characteristics related to hostility, including aggression, altruism, empathy, and trust. What they have learned is directly relevant to the origins of hostility, and it is to their findings that I now turn.

As with many concepts in psychology, a debate exists as to whether those aspects of the personality related to hostility are determined by innate, genetic factors or are learned during the course of development—in other words, whether nature or nurture is more important. Although the pendulum is now swinging in favor of a strong role for the genes, the major early focus was on how one's environment led to more or less trust, more or less altruism or aggression. In the final analysis, it is most likely that how hostile one is will be perceived as resulting from the *interplay* between one's genetic makeup and the environment in which one grows up. The better we understand this interplay, the better equipped we shall be to reduce the toll exacted by hostility upon both our health and our happiness.

HOSTILITY AS A LEARNED PHENOMENON—THE ROLE OF NURTURE

As a first approach, there should be little doubt that hostility *can* be learned. For example, children who are abused by a parent, even a stepparent, are more likely to grow up to abuse their own children, as well as to experience even more wide-ranging problems in controlling their own aggressive tendencies.

In his landmark 1963 book, *Childhood and Society*, Erik Erikson postulated the establishment of a sense of "basic trust" as the first and most important milestone in personality development. If within the first two years of life the individual does not *learn* to trust at least one other person— usually the mother—all subsequent stages of personality development will be impaired.

Trust, and the caregiving that calls it forth, may have emerged on earth with the evolution of mammals. In a lecture delivered to the American Psychiatric Association in 1982, neuroscientist Paul MacLean noted that in contrast to the behavior of reptiles, which may abandon or eat their young, the necessity in mammals for extended nurturant caregiving toward their offspring may have been the evolutionary forerunner of the development of empathy, altruism, conscience, and even social responsibility.

Since newborn offspring need to engage in suckling behavior in order to survive, it also became important that they have the tools essential to find the nipple. And, make no mistake about it, babies are capable of learning, even within the first two hours following birth. After research showed that rats can learn to recognize novel smells while still in the womb and can apply this learning in finding their mother's nipple after birth, Johns Hopkins University researcher Elliott Blass and his colleagues decided to see if newborn human infants are also capable of such learning.

The researchers found that infants two to forty-eight hours old would learn to anticipate a pleasant taste of sucrose. If they stroked a baby's forehead and then placed the sucrose on the tongue, even a two-hour-old infant would soon learn to turn its head in the direction from which the sucrose was always given—in this case, the baby's left side. If the researchers failed to present the sucrose after stroking the forehead, the babies showed their distress: seven out of eight babies cried when the sucrose failed to appear after their foreheads had been stroked. In contrast, only one out of sixteen babies who had not had the sucrose paired with prior stroking of their forehead cried in similar circumstances.

Clearly, then, babies of all mammalian species, up to and including humans, come into the world with the capability of learning how to respond to food-relevant stimuli in ways that bring them closer to the source of nourishment, not to mention—ask any mother—bringing the source of nourishment closer to them! Considering that this nourishment is essential for life itself, it would be surprising indeed if the nature and quality of this most important of all early interactions did not have a profound impact on how one learns to view the world and the people in it.

There is now evidence that, apart from the obvious need for nourishment from the mother, other aspects of the mother-infant interaction also contribute to the infant's growth. Beginning with an accidental finding that rat pups separated from their mothers showed decreased synthesis of new proteins throughout their bodies, Dr. Saul Schanberg, my colleague in Duke's Department of Pharmacology, found that the stunted growth of separated rat pups was not due to lack of nourishment (it occurred too soon), but resulted instead from lack of sensory stimulation of the pups by the mother. In other words, the mother's "tender loving care," in the form of licking her pups, was necessary to maintain sufficient levels of the hormones needed for growth.

This effect has now been shown to apply to human infants as well. Based on Dr. Schanberg's findings, Dr. Tiffany Field of the University of Miami recently demonstrated that frequent stroking of premature infants leads to weight gains that are 47 percent greater than those observed in similar preemies left alone in their incubators—the usual practice. The stroked infants also showed signs of more rapid nervous-system development: they were more active and more responsive to a face or a rattle than the nonstroked preemies.

These research findings demonstrate with remarkable clarity the importance of contact with primary caregivers to the human infant. The infant comes into the world with well-developed capabilities of finding and soliciting nourishment. Beyond such obvious contributions to sustenance, however, it is now evident that touch, loving touch if you will, is also key if the infant is to grow and thrive. Indeed, it was found some years ago, when infants evacuated from the London Blitz were kept in large nurseries, that despite the provision of adequate nourishment, without adequate stimulation from other humans, the babies failed to gain weight and, in many cases, actually wasted away and died.

Yet another study recently completed in rats adds further credence to the impression that early experiences are very important in setting the organism on the path not only to healthy growth and development, but also to coping better with stress later in life. Reported by a team of McGill and Stanford University researchers in the February 12, 1988, issue of *Science,* this study found that rat pups who had been gently handled for fifteen minutes every day from birth to weaning at twenty-two days of age showed much smaller stress hormone responses than did nonhandled rats, even into what, for a rat, is advanced old age— twenty-four months.

These researchers concluded that the stress hormone hypersecretion, brain-cell death, and memory impairments observed in the nonhandled rats ". . . form a complex degenerative cascade of aging in the rat . . . [and] that a subtle manipulation early in life can retard the emergence of this cascade." Future research will attempt to confirm that similar effects occur in human infants and affect stress responses later in life.

All this makes a strong case that environmental factors early in life can have very real effects on both current and later well-being. It's very likely that such factors also influence personality development. More specifically, how infants and children are treated should affect the development of those aspects of hostility that we know to be associated with increased health problems.

THE CASE OF JAPAN

A cross-cultural perspective might best illustrate the different impacts of differences in child-rearing practices. The Japanese psychoanalyst Dr. L. T. Doi has used the concept *amae* to describe what he considers to be a central feature of normal Japanese personality—a kind of dependency on the basic good intentions of others to treat one well and with kindness.

It's revealing that there is no precise equivalent for *amae* in English or any other Western language, and it is obviously quite different from the cynical mistrust I discussed earlier. If *amae* is a basic part of the average Japanese's personality, it follows they should have lower Ho scores than Americans. In a very preliminary look at this question, some of my Japanese colleagues collected Ho scale scores in a sample of Tokyo citizens and found a much larger percentage with low scores than we had found in our patients at Duke. This is being followed up by extensive Ho testing by colleagues in Tokyo, Kyushu, and Sendai. If we find in these much larger samples that scores on the Ho scale and the subgroups we found to predict mortality in the UNC lawyers study are lower in Japan than in U.S. samples with similar backgrounds, it will be strong evidence that Japanese and Americans are fundamentally different when it comes to hostility.

Considerable research into Japanese child-rearing practices points to differences from American practices that could account for hostility differences in adulthood. Doi postulated that the Japanese mother encourages the development of *amae* in her infant by fostering the tendency to seek out the help and support of close individuals and groups.

Studies using close observation of mother-child interactions provided more direct evidence for *amae*-enhancing behaviors on the part of Japanese mothers. Japanese mothers spend little time apart from their children, in contrast to the American mothers, who often depend on baby-sitting. In Japanese families, close physical contact is seen as a natural expression of affection, necessary and proper for the rearing of children. Even in matters of discipline, the Japanese mother was seen as placing a higher value on the preservation of closeness between herself and the child than on absolute obedience. Consequently, it seems that a guiding principle for Japanese mothers is never to go against the child; instead, Japanese mothers work very hard to avoid expressing negative emotions toward or about the child, even when he or she misbehaves. They never embarrass or ridicule their children, though they may warn them that *others* will do so if they continue to behave in a certain way.

Indeed, many investigators have noted that the basic orientation toward the child in Japan is that he or she is good, wonderful, clever, and the like, rather than inherently bad, or laden, as some Western thought would maintain, with original sin. The Japanese mother's efforts are directed toward training her children in proper interpersonal relationships, rather than emphasizing only the achievement and status of her children.

In a classic study supported by the National Institute of Mental Health in the early 1960s, Dr. William Caudill and his associates at the Laboratory of Socio-environmental Studies, NIMH, spent months observing mother-infant interactions in Japanese and American homes. In contrast to American mothers, who let the infant cry though they hovered close by, Japanese mothers picked up the baby and comforted it at the first cry. Whereas American mothers relied more on verbal modes of interaction—they talked more to their babies—Japanese mothers tended to emphasize close physical contact.

In follow-up studies of these infants at ages 2 and 6 years, compared to the Japanese children, the American children were seen as "more active, more vocally and physically emotional, more independent, and more likely to manipulate functionally both their social and physical environment"—not bad characteristics, but acquired, perhaps, at the cost of the high levels of trust imparted to Japanese children.

Since other studies, of American mothers of Japanese

ancestry, showed them to treat their children much the same as the American mothers studied earlier by Caudill, it appears that these Japanese-American differences in maternal behavior toward the child are culturally rather than genetically determined.

Direct evidence that Japanese mothers are more likely in general to use appeals for empathy rather than assertions of their own authority in obtaining compliance in their children came from an interesting study of how long it took 11-month-old infants to resume movement toward a new toy following their mother's utterance of an *angry* vocal expression. American infants studied in Denver, Colorado, resumed locomotion toward the toy within 17.5 seconds following their mother's angry vocalization. In striking contrast, it took nearly 49 seconds before the Japanese infants, studied in Sapporo, Hokkaido, started moving again after their mother's angry command. The researchers' interpretation of this difference: By 11 months of age, the Japanese infants had experienced such vocalizations much less frequently than had their American counterparts, so that when they heard an angry voice, it had more impact.

I have dwelt at length on this research because some of the distinctive characteristics of Japanese child-rearing practices seem almost designed to induce higher levels of interpersonal trust among the Japanese. The designation of the term *amae* to describe a central aspect of the typical Japanese personality, coupled with the preliminary finding of lower Ho scores in Japan, suggests that Japanese child-rearing practices do have the expected behavioral effects.

Thus, it does appear to matter, with respect to hostility levels among adults, how children are treated. The Japanese data suggest that when children are regarded as good, provided with much loving physical contact, and seldom exposed to angry expressions, they grow up to be more trusting and to work hard to maintain good relationships. This is all-important because it suggests that changes in *our* child-rearing practices might be one means of reducing hostility in Western cultures.

HOW WE GET WHAT WE EXPECT: THE SELF-FULFILLING PROPHECY

Lest there be any lingering doubts that how we treat other people, including children, can exert strong influences on the behavior of others, let me describe some research that demonstrates the power of expectations to affect others' behavior.

As put by Edward Jones of Princeton University in an article published in the October 3, 1986, issue of *Science*, "We are not passive observers of our respective social worlds, but active forces in the shaping of those worlds. To an important extent we create our own social reality by influencing the behavior we observe in others." While the work that supports this point has been done largely in adults, it is easy to see that such effects would be even more profound and long-lasting among infants when the source of the social influence is their parents.

The power of our expectations to influence the behavior of others was demonstrated in a somewhat controversial experiment in 1968 (described in Jones's *Science* article) in which teachers were led to expect that certain of their students (who had actually been selected at random) were destined to "bloom" academically. Subsequent objective testing showed that these students actually performed better than students who had not been so designated. Even though they were operating on the basis of an incorrect expectation, even though they were unaware that they had done anything themselves to create the end result, the teachers somehow behaved in such a way that their expectation of students' performance became reality. As Jones noted, this kind of result confirms the essence of the "self-fulfilling prophecy."

One additional example of this principle that "we make happen what we expect to happen" will serve to make the point. In another study described by Jones, fifty-one male university undergraduates took part in an experiment in which their task was to have a "get acquainted" telephone conversation with fifty-one female undergraduates. Before making the call, each male subject was shown a snapshot, allegedly of the woman he was about to call, leading half to believe that she was very beautiful, while the other half got the impression that the woman to whom they would soon be speaking was downright ugly. The female subjects did not know about these snapshots, and, in fact, the pictures had been randomly assigned to the male subjects, without any relationship to the woman actually being called.

Again, the self-fulfilling prophecy came to pass. Independent observers who knew nothing of the snapshots rated the men who had been shown the attractive pictures as more friendly, open, and sociable than those who had received the unattractive pictures. Another group of judges, who listened only to the female side of the conversations, judged the women in the "attractive" condition to be more poised, sociable, gregarious, and self-confident than the women who were talking to men operating under the impression they were not attractive.

If even such casual telephone interactions can so influence the behavior one expects of others, then how much more profound must be the influence of a parent's expectations regarding his or her children?

The child-parent relationship aside, how do our expectations of others influence and reinforce their behavior toward us?

The answer, I believe, lies in the expression of our expectations, and the emotions they engender, in the face we present to the world. Darwin was the first to call attention to the universality with which certain basic emotions—anger, joy, fear, disgust, contempt, surprise, sadness, and the like—are manifested in the facial expressions of both humans and animals. More recently, researchers like Paul Ekman of the University of California in San Francisco have documented that all human cultures, even preliterate ones, can recognize and agree upon the facial expressions representing these emotions. Such findings indicate that emotional expressions are not artifacts of different cultures, but are really biologically adaptive signals with an evolutionary history.

These profoundly strong signals are effective in communicating our emotions and expectations to others. Think of how you feel when around someone who always seems to have a "sourpuss" expression. Do you begin to feel down yourself, or angry and irritated? Might you wind up confirming the sourpuss's "expectation" of you as a result?

Imagine, if you will, how a parent whose facial expression nearly always carries signs of anger and/or disgust will affect the behavior of the dependent child who looks to that parent as the source of all sustenance. Think of how *your* facial expressions may have affected the moods and behavior of your own children, or of how your parents' facial expressions may have played a role in the development of your own expectancies about the world and the people in it.

It is possible, even when we are not consciously aware of experiencing an emotion, for that emotion to be evident in our face. For example, when a hostile person is waiting in a line that is moving too slowly, his or her face will often show his anger and disgust even before awareness of the emotions reaches his consciousness.

Do the faces of hostile persons show negative emotions more than nonhostile individuals? Research carried out by Margaret Chesney and Paul Ekman suggests that they do.

Without being aware of whether the subjects were Type A or B, Ekman rated the facial expressions of men who had undergone the Type A structured interview. The largest difference between them was the more frequent and intense expression of *disgust* in the Type A men.

The most direct evidence concerning the possible role of parenting behaviors in the development of Type A behavior and hostility in children comes from research conducted by Dr. Karen Matthews and her coworkers at the University of Pittsburgh. In these studies, mothers of Type A children were observed to make less frequent positive remarks about their children's performance on an achievement task and to encourage them to try harder even when they did well on the task. Parents of Type A children were also more likely to make critical remarks than parents of Type B children. Fathers of Type A boys were observed to use more physical and restrictive discipline techniques, while fathers of Type B boys were more likely to explain the reasons behind the discipline.

Focusing directly on the sorts of family environments that might be conducive to the development of hostility and anger, Dr. Matthews and her associate Dr. Karen Woodall found that the more hostile and angry children came from families whose scores on questionnaires indicated that the family was less cohesive, less supportive, less open to expression of feelings, and less actively involved in their social environments than families whose children were less hostile and angry. Based on such evidence, they suggest that hostile, angry children may well be the product of families that are less supportive, less open with their feelings, less positively involved with their children, and more likely to use physical and restrictive techniques in disciplining their children. On the other hand, parents' high expectations may contribute to high ambition in Type As.

There is ample evidence, therefore, for the role of environment, of how we treat our children, as a strong determinant of various aspects of hostility. In his book *Treating Type A and Your Heart*, Meyer Friedman points to the importance, in fostering various aspects of Type A behavior, of ". . . the failure of the Type A person in his infancy and very early childhood to receive *unconditional* love, affection, and encouragement from one or both of his parents." What research teaches us about ways in which this influence is exerted can be used (as we shall learn in part 2) to devise approaches that could help reduce the hostility we impart to children.

So much for "nurture." What about "nature"—do the genes have any role to play in a hostile attitude?

HOSTILITY AS AN INNATE PHENOMENON: THE ROLE OF NATURE

Of course they do. The evidence that is now mounting regarding the heritability of hostility and related traits, such as altruism and aggression, will increase our understanding of how environmental influences can be themselves affected by the genetic makeup of the individual, as well as how hostility and its genetic underpinnings might lead to disease.

The degree to which behavioral traits can be influenced by one's genetic makeup can only be described as amazing. In a University of Minnesota study of identical twins separated at birth and reared apart—an important means of ruling out environmental influences, since identical twins in the same family might be treated very similarly—researchers have been continually struck by the range of characteristics that are similar in the twins.

Two male twins in their late forties, one raised in Germany as a Catholic and one raised a Jew in Trinidad, both took a strange delight in surprising people by sneezing in elevators. Other examples abound: separated twins who each have a circular bench around a tree in their backyard; both twins wearing the same number of rings on each hand, and on each finger.

While the notion that behavioral tendencies can be inherited in humans flies in the face of many egalitarian ideals and raises fears of biological determinism, it cannot be ignored that, just as with eye color, body build, tendencies toward baldness, and a host of other "physical" characteristics, one's psychological makeup is also very much a product of one's genes.

In the Minnesota study, numerous personality traits were found to be about 50 percent explainable by the genetic similarity. Even social attitudes that would seem to fall more in the realm of things one learns showed strong genetic inputs. Thus, whether one is conservative or liberal on the political spectrum was determined to be about 50 percent due to one's genes.

Since the relationship of the traits in identical twins reared apart was nearly as strong as that in twins reared together, researchers have been forced to conclude that the environment shared by twins raised in the same family had little or no role in producing whatever personality similarities they had. In other words, the genetic makeup and the influence it had upon each twin's interaction with the environment was more important in making identical twins' personalities similar than the fact that they were raised in the same family.

As to the traits that concern us here, measures of altruism, empathy, nurturance, aggressiveness, and assertiveness have all been found to show strong, clear-cut genetic influences. Again, the shared environment of the twins contributed relatively little to their similarities in these traits.

In addition to the studies on hostility-related traits, preliminary studies by several behavioral geneticists are finding that scores on the Ho scale, as well as some of the subscales (like the cynicism subgroup of items) that appear important in predicting increased risk of disease, are influenced as much by genes as by environment.

While it is now clear, and generally accepted by most experts in this field, that genes contribute as much to personality as environment, it is far less clear—murky would not be an overstatement—what mechanisms are accounting for the genetic influences. We can now show, using the twin approach, that these traits are inherited, but we have no real indications as to what biological characteristics—which chemicals, which hormones, neurotransmitters, and the like—are encoded by the genes that make one more or less aggressive, altruistic, or trusting.

At present, the best we can do is speculate. Fortunately, some clues from research in animals already exist that may lead us in the right direction.

An extensive body of research on negative personality traits, such as hostility, aggression, and cynicism, shows that aggressive behaviors, studied mostly in rats, are affected by changes in various neurotransmitters in the brain. A neurotransmitter is a chemical that is released by a nerve ending, crosses over to another tissue close by, attaches to a receptor, and causes a series of changes within the cells of the target tissue. We have already discussed this concept in talking about norepinephrine as a messenger for the emergency branch of the autonomic nervous system. In similar fashion, norepinephrine is one of many neurotransmitters used by nerve cells in the brain to communicate with one another.

During my research training at the National Institute of Mental Health (NIMH) in the early 1970s, I worked in the same lab with another trainee, Dr. Burr Eichelman, an M.D./Ph.D. from Chicago whose Ph.D. research had concentrated on the brain systems that control aggression in the rat. At NIMH, Burr extended this work to include evaluating the effect of changes in various brain neuro-transmitter systems upon aggressive behavior in rats. Burr found that when drugs increased norepinephrine activity, heightened aggression resulted. In contrast, there were drugs that acted on other brain neurotransmitter systems to reduce aggressive behavior. The *benzodiazepines* (e.g., Valium, Librium, and Xanax) affected GABA (gamma-amino-buturic acid—another neurotransmitter) systems: Burr found that the drugs' sedating action diminished aggressive behavior in rats. Another class of drugs that decreases aggressive behavior are the *opioids* (e.g., morphine, codeine, and heroin). These act upon opiate receptors in the brain to reduce pain, enhance pleasure, reduce activity in the emergency branch, and enhance activity in the calming branch of the autonomic nervous system.

Since all of these drugs act upon naturally occurring biologic mechanisms in the brain, it seems likely that the genetic influences upon personality act through related neurotransmitter systems or their receptors. For example, if the gene that makes the enzyme that produces an aggression-modulating neurotransmitter is set to make more or less of that substance in a given individual, it could lead to differences in aggressive behaviors.

On a more positive note, Bowling Green State University psychologist Jaak Panksepp has proposed an interesting speculative hypothesis to explain the neurobiological determinants of altruism—the tendency to help others. Endogenous opioidlike substances, or "endorphins," are the normal stimulators of the brain's opioid receptors. Endorphins are released when the organism is stressed acutely. Their pain-relieving effects explain why soldiers who have had limbs mutilated in battle may not experience pain.

Panksepp believes that activation of brain opioid systems by social stimulation may be one means whereby social bonding and hence tendencies to altruism may be encouraged. Although he acknowledges that this is really no more than a speculative theory at present, the evidence Panksepp advances in its support is quite interesting in its implications for how the inheritance of hostility might also be accomplished.

In studies with both chicks and rat pups, Panksepp has found that blockade of the opioid receptors with the antagonist drug naloxone results in more distress vocalizations ("peeps and squeaks") when young animals are separated from the flock or litter. Play behavior, which requires a certain amount of "trust" between the two baby animals, is also reduced by naloxone treatment, and nerve activity increases in brain opioid systems when animals are playing. Conversely, treatment with opioid-receptor stimulants, like morphine, reduces distress vocalizations and increases play behavior.

Based on such observations, Panksepp suggests that "brain opioids, which promote social comfort, bonding, and play, presumably evoke psychological attitudes of peacefulness and trust." In contrast, opioid withdrawal would promote distress, irritability, and aggression. Mammalian helping behaviors (altruism), Panksepp feels, may arise from the negative and positive effects, respectively, of separation from the mother versus experience of maternal nurturance—effects that are mediated by withdrawal or stimulation of opioid release.

If one's genes are such that the enzyme "machinery" that makes endorphins is set at a relatively low level, the result would be little social comfort when in contact with the mother or other animals: being with other animals/ people would have little to offer such an organism in the way of positive reinforcement, since the contact does not lead to much of an increase in endorphin stimulation. In animals with a more fully developed opioid-manufacturing system, however, social contacts would be very reinforcing, leading the organism to like being with others and to do those things, presumably "altruistic," that would increase the likelihood of social contacts.

Similarly, the infant or small child whose endorphin system really fires off in the presence of parents or other kids learns to connect the presence of others with pleasurable feelings. Besides increasing his or her desire for the company of others, these pleasurable feelings are likely to lead such a child to conclude in addition that other people are good. As we saw earlier, it would also then be likely that the child's expectations that others are good would probably encourage those others to in fact treat the child better.

Just how might the genes conversely lead to higher levels of cynical mistrust? Recall that hostile people appear to have less robust—and nonhostile people, more robust—calming-branch responses. It is known, from research in animals, that opioids can protect the heart against the effects of excessive emergency-branch stimulation. This protective effect of opioids is mediated through activation of the calming branch of the autonomic nervous system. Other evidence shows that many of the effects of opioids on heart and blood vessel function result from activation of the calming branch.

These points, taken together, begin to dovetail nicely here. It is possible to make up a quite plausible story—still speculative—that hostility, or at least many of its aspects, could be inherited as the following review indicates:

1. The genes make fewer opioid neurotransmitters (e.g., endorphins).

2. This causes fewer opioid receptors to be stimulated during social contacts and, as one of many consequences, the calming branch is slower to turn on and stop the effects of the emergency-branch activation stimulated by the same social contacts. As another consequence, less pleasure is experienced from the social contacts.

3. By virtue of the more prolonged emergency-branch activation, which is experienced as unpleasant after a

while, and by virtue of the absence of pleasurable feelings, the child with the "low-endorphin genes" does not derive comfort from contacts with parents or others and even experiences such contacts, if prolonged, as unpleasant.

4. Being a rational animal, the child sees the connections between his or her unpleasant feelings and the circumstances in which they occur and draws the conclusion—"learns"—that rather than being the source of basically positive things, people are the source of unpleasant feelings.

5. Given such feelings, the child behaves in ways—puts on facial expressions of anger and disgust; squirms and cries a lot when held; doesn't seem outgoing with strangers—that cause others to withdraw, to actually be less kind; to, as Edward Jones pointed out, fulfill the child's prophecy that others are not so nice to be around.

The scenario I just outlined must be corroborated by much further research before it can be accepted as *the* explanation of how hostility is inherited and then further established by one's environment. That research is going on right now, and I hope this book will encourage even more of it. Some of this research already supports the scenario.

For several decades, first at Fels Research Institute in Yellow Springs, Ohio, and now at Harvard University, Dr. Jerome Kagan has been studying differences in the temperament of children. "Temperament" refers to stable individual differences in the timing and intensity of emotional arousal and expression. Many researchers feel that temperament is genetically determined and may be an important influence on parent-child interactions. The focus of much of Dr. Kagan's attention has been on the temperamental disposition of *inhibition.*

Inhibition refers to the tendency evident in the first year of life and thereafter for the child to stop playing, become quiet, even to assume a wary facial expression, when presented with a stranger, a novel stimulus of some sort, or an unfamiliar peer or event. Such temperamental inhibition is consistently present in about 10 percent of American two-year-olds. In contrast to inhibited children, other infants quickly smile, talk to an adult stranger, and even play with the stranger for a few seconds. *Shy, cautious,* and *timid* are the terms parents use to describe their inhibited children, whereas parents of uninhibited children use terms like *sociable, bold, exploratory,* or *fearless.*

Dr. Kagan has not neglected the physiological aspects of inhibition in his research. His findings are remarkably consistent with the postulated consequences of having the "low-endorphin gene." According to Kagan's research, inhibited children show higher levels of emergency-branch activation, especially under conditions of behavioral stress. Their heart rate is fast and steady and does not vary much as they breathe in and out. These are both signs of increased emergency-branch and diminished calming-branch activity.

So there is at least some indication that shy, inhibited children are characterized not only by apparent discomfort during social contacts but also by a diminished calming-branch antagonism of prolonged emergency-branch activity. It is tempting to surmise that at least one reason why these children find strange situations distressing is that their emergency-branch activation in such circumstances is not terminated by the calming branch kicking in to cool things down, but continues and continues, until it becomes unpleasant. Whether their relatively weak calming-branch response is genetically determined, and related to inadequate opioid receptor stimulation, will remain questions for further research.

A related question that Dr. Kagan may be able to answer as he continues to follow the children he has already studied and characterized as inhibited or uninhibited is whether as they mature the inhibited children will become the ones with high Ho scores, especially high scores on the Cynicism, Angry Feelings, Aggressive Responding subgroups that predict higher mortality rates in young adulthood to midlife.

Hostility begins before birth, its precursors contained within our genes. However, our experiences can have a major impact on our hostility levels, though those caring for us may have to overcome the influences of the genes on our behavior to provide the kind of care that will lead to less hostile, more trusting children and adults. Dr. Kagan's research is already finding that inhibited children may become more or less shy as they grow older, depending upon the presence or absence of such environmental factors as prolonged hospitalization, death of a parent, marital discord, and the like.

As we learn more, this knowledge will help us to devise better approaches to child rearing, approaches that could diminish the expression of the genetic predisposition to hostility. We may also be able to use new knowledge regarding the biological mediators of hostility to reduce both maladaptive hostility and its adverse effects on health.

I have told you here what is known about the origins of hostility within an individual. Next, I want to share with you the idea that what we have learned from research about hostility and its converse, the trusting heart, may have parallels in human knowledge that goes back more than two thousand years.

SEVEN

PARALLELS IN WORLD RELIGIONS: ANCIENT TRUTH AND MODERN PROOF

Characteristics describing the trusting heart emerged from meticulous analyses of psychological test items that epidemiological research had shown to predict higher versus lower coronary heart disease and mortality rates. As revealed by these analyses, the trusting heart believes others are basically good, is slow to anger, and treats others with considerate kindness. I have been struck by the similarity between the trusting heart and what I know of the "Golden Rule" so common in many of the world's religions.

I am certainly no theologian, and I make no claim here to have undertaken a scholarly study of world religions. But I have attempted to familiarize myself with the teachings of some of the major religions, using both scriptures and secondary sources, to see whether some of these teachings point in the same direction as the research on hostility and disease—toward the benefits of having a trusting heart. Diverse as they are, several of the world's major religions contain a central tenet that bears a striking resemblance to the picture of the trusting heart that has emerged from modern research.

Read on without skipping any of the religions I review here, and perhaps you will be convinced, as I have been, that, in this case at least, science and religion lead us to the same place.

CHRISTIANITY

Jesus taught that we should love God, and that we should also love our neighbor as much as we love ourself; an idea perhaps best expressed in Luke:

> And behold, a lawyer stood up to put him to the test, saying, "Teacher, what shall I do to inherit eternal life?" He said to him, "What is written in the law? How do you read?" And he answered, "You shall love the Lord your God with all your heart, and with all your soul, and with all your strength, and with all your mind; and your neighbor as yourself." And he said to him, "You have answered right; do this, and you will live." (10:25–28)

This was elaborated further when the lawyer went on to ask, "Who is my neighbor?" and Jesus replied with the parable of the Good Samaritan, in which he suggested that even those considered outcasts by society should be considered as our neighbor. Jesus went still further, admonishing each of us to go beyond loving those who love us, but also to

Love your enemies, do good to those who hate you, bless those who curse you, pray for those who abuse you. To him who strikes you on the cheek, offer the other also; and from him who takes away your cloak do not withold your coat as well. . . . And as you wish that men would do to you, do so to them. (Luke 6:27–29, 31)

Jesus described God not as some impersonal force of nature, but as a loving father, one to whom he referred as "Abba," the Aramaic word for "Papa." Just as God has clothed so well the lilies of the field, so also will he take care to clothe us (Matthew 6:25, 28–30). And just as any of us will not give our son a stone when he asks for bread, ". . . how much more will your Father who is in heaven give good things to those who ask Him!" (Matthew 7:9–11).

When asked by the Pharisees when the kingdom of God was coming, Jesus replied that it is not going to be heralded by observable signs; ". . . nor will they say, 'Lo, here it is!' or 'There!' for behold, the kingdom of God is within you" (Luke 17:20–21).

You probably already see many parallels between these teachings and the research findings described earlier regarding those personal characteristics conducive to a healthier, longer life. Let me point to a few that seem particularly important.

In contrast to the hostile heart, for whom everyone is an "enemy" at some time or another, the trusting heart believes in the basic goodness of humankind. In contrast to the hostile heart—which does not bother to hide its poor opinion of another to spare his or her feelings, which does not refrain from being rough with those who are rude, which likes to get even with those who have done it a wrong—the trusting heart treats others well, with consideration and kindness. This seems to me very much like loving one's neighbor—perhaps even one's enemies—as oneself.

In his first letter to the Corinthians, the Apostle Paul emphasized the central importance of love and provided us with more explicit descriptions of what Jesus meant by love. We might have all wisdom, be able to express ourselves with the utmost eloquence, even be able to move mountains with our faith, Paul says; but if we have not love, we are nothing (I Corinthians 13:1–2). Paul's description of the characteristics of love bears a striking resemblance to the characteristics of the trusting heart that emerged from the epidemiological research cited earlier:

> Love is patient and kind; love is not jealous or boastful; it is not arrogant or rude. Love does not insist on its own way; it is not irritable or resentful; it does not rejoice in the wrong, but rejoices in the right. Love bears all things, believes all things, hopes all things, endures all things. (I Corinthians 13:4–7)

For Jesus, when human beings' lives are characterized by this kind of love, the kingdom of God is realized, not at some future apocalyptic end of the world, but here and now in today's world. But to have such love is not easy. It may require us to put away our suspicions and mistrust of human motives. Jesus suggests this when he says, ". . . unless you turn and become like children, you will never enter the kingdom of heaven" (Matthew 18:3). To believe and to hope truly, we must adopt a childlike trust in the basic goodness of others—an attitude, by the way, not unlike the *amae* I noted earlier to be a characteristic of Japanese children whose mothers protected them from all frustrations.

What parallels can be drawn between Jesus' teachings and the research on the biological underpinnings of hostility? When the lawyer asked how he could achieve "eternal life," Jesus told him that if he loves God and his neighbor as himself, he "will live" (Luke 10:28). We infer that Jesus was referring here to an afterlife. The experimental laboratory research on the trusting heart has identified biological characteristics of those who trust others, experience little anger, and treat others with kindness that appear to confer some protection against premature illness and death. Both Jesus' teaching and the epidemiological research findings appear to be making a similar point: if we love others, our "life"—by either definition—will be increased.

And what of the research suggesting that a more robust endorphin response to being with other people may be a genetically determined biological characteristic predisposing us to be more trusting of others? Jesus' position that "the kingdom of God is within you" suggests there may be something within each human that moves us to love our neighbor. Another parallel can be found in John's statement that "God is love, and he who abides in love abides in God and God abides in him" (I John 4:16). Research on the trusting heart suggests that *within* our biological makeup there may be physiological mechanisms that predispose us to trust others and treat them well.

But parallels between religion and research on the trusting heart are not confined to Christianity.

JUDAISM

When Jesus asked the lawyer, "What is the law?" he was referring to the Torah, or Written Law, which God had delivered to Moses—that is, the Ten Commandments plus many additional rules found throughout the first five books of the Bible—and to the Oral Law, or "Sayings of the Fathers," also known as the "Pirke Aboth," a collection of legal principles and devotional or ethical interpretations handed down from the fourth century B.C.E. onward.

The injunction to love one's neighbor as oneself and the conception that one's neighbors are all humankind can be found in Leviticus:

> You shall not take vengeance or bear any grudge against the sons of your own people, but you shall love your neighbor as yourself. (19:18)

> When a stranger sojourns with you in your land, you shall not do him wrong. The stranger who sojourns with you shall be to you as the native among you, and you shall love him as yourself, for you were strangers in the land of Egypt. (19:33, 34)

In his commentary on the *Sayings of the Fathers*, Chief Rabbi of the British Empire Joseph Hertz illustrated the central importance of the "Golden Rule" among the hundreds of rules and laws in the Torah by relating the story of Hillel's reply to the heathen scoffer who challenged him to summarize the whole Torah in a single sentence. Hillel, the most renowned of the Rabbis for his humility and kindness, was active from 30 B.C.E. to 10 of the Common Era. To the scoffer's question he replied, "Whatever is hateful unto thee, do it not unto thy fellow: this is the whole Torah; the rest is explanation."

A central tenet of Judaism, then, is that we should love all humankind and treat them as we ourselves would wish to be treated. This, too, parallels the findings of the research on the trusting heart, and is illustrated further and more explicitly in other parts of the *Sayings of the Fathers*.

Rabbi Joshua ben Chananya, who lived toward the end of the first century of the Common Era, is credited with saying, "The evil eye, the evil inclination, and hatred of his fellow-creatures drive a man out of the world" (II-16). If the "evil eye" refers to the opposite of the "good eye," the latter being able to see the good in other people, we might interpret this saying to suggest that a cynical view of others, anger toward others, and evil treatment of others will shorten one's life.

Another parallel between our modern research and the teachings of Judaism is made explicit in the following, a description of those whose study of the Torah has imbued them with the qualities of love of God and man, cheerfulness, love of mercy, truthfulness, humility, and peacefulness:

> For they are life unto those that find them, and health to all their flesh; and it says, It shall be healthy to thy navel, and marrow to thy bones; and it says, It is a tree of life to them that grasp it. . . . For by me thy days shall be multiplied, and the years of thy life shall be increased. . . . For length of days, and years of life, and peace shall they add to thee. (VI-7)

This faith also has relevant observations to make concerning the importance of controlling our anger. One of Rabbi Joshua ben Chananya's disciples, Rabbi Simeon ben Zoma, emphasized it this way:

> Who is mighty? He who subdues his passions; as it is said, He that is slow to anger is better than the mighty, and he that ruleth over his spirit than he that taketh a city. (IV-1)

In another Chapter of the Sayings, Rabbi Meir points out that anyone—that is, not only Jews—who obeys the Law of God will garner many attributes that today appear similar to those shown by research to characterize those with a trusting heart:

> He is called friend, beloved, a lover of the All-present, a lover of mankind: it clothes him in meekness and reverence . . . he is made like a never-failing fountain, and like

a river that flows on with ever-sustained vigor; he becomes modest, patient, and forgiving of insults; and it magnifies and exalts him above all things. (VI-1)

BUDDHISM

Just as Christianity grew out of the teachings of a man named Jesus who was seen as the messiah, or "Christ," so also has Buddhism grown out of the teachings of a man named Siddhārtha Gautama who was seen as the "enlightened one," or "Buddha." Born of noble parents in northeast India about 563 B.C.E., as a young man Gautama was touched by the human suffering he saw around him and embarked upon a search for the truth that would relieve this suffering.

After six years of wandering, meditation, and self-mortification, Gautama resolved at the start of one evening to sit at the base of a *bodhi* tree and not rise until he had attained enlightenment. He was assaulted by Mara, the evil one, or tempter, who is lord of the world of passion, who sought to defeat him and keep him from enlightenment. Supported by the ten virtues he had perfected in past lives as a *bodhisattva* ("Buddha-to-be"), Gautama meditated through the night and defeated Mara. By morning he had attained enlightenment, or *Nirvana;* Gautama was now the Buddha.

Soon thereafter, the Buddha preached his first sermon, "Setting in Motion the Wheel of Truth," to a small group of disciples in a village near the present city of Benares. In this sermon he revealed to them the four noble truths. The first noble truth is that man's existence is full of conflict, dissatisfaction, sorrow, and suffering. The second is that this suffering originates in our own selfish desire or craving for pleasure; the third, that there is a means whereby this craving and the suffering it causes can be eliminated. The fourth noble truth is that the way to this liberation—to Nirvana—is the Noble Eightfold Path consisting of right view, right thought, right speech, right action, right mode of livelihood, right effort, right mindfulness, and right concentration.

As with Christianity and Judaism, there are many parallels between the Buddha's teachings and what we have learned from research on the relationship between hostility and disease. One that comes quickly to mind is suggested by the second noble truth, the notion that harm comes from our involvement with our self—the delusion of ego that determines our craving for pleasure, our concern with our existence and nonexistence. (Recall the research of Dr. Larry Scherwitz, who found that the more self-involved his research subjects—as indexed by the use of personal pronouns like "I," "me," and "mine"—the larger were their blood-pressure responses to laboratory tasks, and the more likely were they to have severe coronary arteriosclerosis or suffer a heart attack.)

Among the Six Perfections that must be mastered to become a *bodhisattva,* the last is the Perfection of Wisdom, which holds up the ideal of the utter negation of self:

> . . . form is emptiness and the very emptiness is form; emptiness does not differ from form, nor does form differ from emptiness; whatever is form, that is emptiness, whatever is emptiness, that is form. The same is true of feelings, perceptions, impulses, and consciousness.

> . . . owing to a Bodhisattva's indifference to any kind of personal attainment, and through his having relied on the Perfection of Wisdom [*Prajnaparamita*], he dwells without thought-coverings. . . . Therefore, one should know the *Prajnaparamita* as the great spell, the spell of great knowledge, the utmost spell, the unequalled spell,

allayer of all suffering . . . By the *Prajnaparamita* has this spell been delivered. It turns like this: Gone, Gone, gone beyond, gone altogether beyond, O what an awakening, all hail! *(Prajnaparamitahvdaya-Sutra)*

Many other parallels can be found upon examination of Buddhist teachings relating to the Eightfold Path as the way to Nirvana. For example, right thought is said to consist of thoughts that are free from desire, free from ill will, and free from cruelty. Right speech is not that which is false, lying, or harsh, but, rather, that which spreads concord and amity—words that are gentle, soothing to the ear, loving, courteous, friendly, and agreeable to many. Right action is not only the abstention from such evil acts as killing and stealing, but also consists of the more positive virtues of conscientiousness, sympathy, and concern for the welfare of all living beings.

Among the ideals portrayed in the Buddhist text *Majjhima-Nikaya* is the following, a description of the four "Sublime Abodes" of love, compassion, sympathetic joy, and equanimity wherein the monk is admonished to dwell:

Having his mind accompanied by love he abides . . . pervading the entire world with his mind accompanied by love, with abundant, great, immeasurable freedom from hatred and malice. Having his mind accompanied by compassion he abides . . . accompanied by sympathetic joy . . . by equanimity, with abundant, great, immeasurable freedom from hatred and malice. (*Majjhima-Nikaya*, I, 281)

Love, or *metta*, to use the Indo-Aryan word, in the Buddhist sense is not so much ordinary human affection as an impartial benevolence directed toward all living beings. Without it, the other Sublime Abodes—Compassion, Sympathetic Joy, and Equanimity—are incomplete. Thus, without love *(metta)*, Compassion will turn to contempt, Sympathetic Joy to vicarious satisfaction, and Equanimity to heartless indifference. It is not hard to see a latter-day connection between this kind of love and a trusting heart.

The *bodhisattva* ideal, too, provides a parallel between Buddhist teachings and the descriptions of the trusting heart that have come from modern epidemiological research. By the true practice of the Six Perfections *(Paramita)*—generosity, morality, patience, vigor, concentration, and wisdom—anyone, not just a monk, may generate within one's own self the thought of Enlightenment and thus approach the state of being a Buddha.

The Six Perfections themselves suggest many parallels with the trusting heart.

In Buddhism, generosity, for example, generalizes one's natural affections to all living beings, even animals. Giving is practiced not for the sake of acquiring merits, or of gaining individual salvation, but in order to bring Enlightenment to all sentient beings.

The Perfection of Patience, which includes not only the literal meanings of patience and forbearance, but also love, humility, endurance, absence of anger or desire for retaliation and revenge—many characteristics that are illustrated in the Ho scale to describe the trusting heart—invites some particularly interesting comparisons. Not only parallels with the trusting heart, but also parallels between Jesus' teachings are embodied in the Perfection of Patience, exemplified here by the Parable of the Saw, in which the Buddha says:

> When men speak evil of ye, thus may ye train yourselves: "Our heart shall be unwavering, no evil word will we send forth, but compassionate of others' welfare will we abide, of kindly heart without resentment: and that man who thus speaks will we suffuse with thoughts accompanied by love, and so abide: and, making that our stand-

point, we will suffuse the whole world with loving thoughts, far-reaching, wide-spreading, boundless, free from hate, free from ill-will, and so abide." Thus, brethren, must ye train yourselves.

Moreover, brethren, though robbers, who are highwaymen, should with a two-handed saw carve you in pieces limb by limb, yet if the mind of any one of you should be offended thereat, such an one is no follower of my gospel. (*Majjhima-Nikaya*, I, 128–29)

CONFUCIANISM

Born in 551 B.C.E., Confucius educated himself so diligently that he became the most learned man of his day. But of even greater concern to him, however, was the misery he saw all about him. Like Gautama, Confucius dedicated his life to finding solutions to the problems of human suffering. During the nearly twenty-five hundred years since his death, Confucius's teachings have been both a religion and a way of life for the Chinese people, as well as the people of other Asian countries that borrowed their culture from China.

Just as the Gospels of the New Testament provide the most reliable source of information on the life and teachings of Jesus, so does the *Lun yu* ("Conversations"), or the *Analects*, constitute the basic scripture of Confucianism. The central concept in Confucius's teachings is denoted by the Chinese character *jen*, and as we'll see, this reminds us of the research on the trusting heart in a number of ways.

Among the English words used by translators to convey the meaning of *jen* are: *good* (in the broadest and most general sense); *virtue; love; magnanimity;* and *human-hearted-*

ness. When asked about *jen* by his disciples, Confucius's briefest answer was "Love men."

I can think of no better way to illustrate the parallels between the teachings of Confucius and what research has taught us about the characteristics of the trusting heart than simply to quote for you several passages from the *Analects.*

> The Master said, Shen! My Way has one [thread] that runs right through it. Master Tseng said, Yes. When the Master had gone out, the disciples asked, saying What did he mean? Master Tseng said, Our Master's Way is simply this: Loyalty, consideration [for the feelings of others, "not doing to them anything one would not like to have done to oneself"]. (IV, 15)

> Tzu-kung asked saying, Is there any single saying that one can act upon all day and every day? The Master said, Perhaps the saying about consideration: "Never do to others what you would not like them to do to you." (XV, 23)

> The Master said, [the good man] does not grieve that other people do not recognize his merits. His only anxiety is lest he should fail to recognize theirs. (I, 16)

> The Master said, If out of the three hundred *Songs* I had to take one phrase to cover all my teaching, I would say "Let there be no evil in your thoughts." (II, 2)

> . . . the Master said, He whose heart is in the smallest degree set upon Goodness will dislike no one. (IV, 4)

> The Master said, If a man has gifts as wonderful as those of the Duke of Chou, yet is arrogant and mean, all the rest is of no account. (VIII, 11)

> The Master said, The gentleman calls attention to the good points in others; he does not call attention to their defects. The small man does just the reverse of this. (XII, 16)

Fan Ch'ih asked about Goodness. The Master said, In private life, courteous, in public life, diligent, in relationships, loyal. This is a maxim that no matter where you may be, even amid the barbarians of the east or north, may never be set aside. (XIII, 19)

Tzu-kung was always criticizing other people. The Master said, It is fortunate for Tzu that he is so perfect himself as to have time to spare for this. I myself have none. (XIV, 31)

The Master said, Is it the man who "does not count beforehand upon the falsity of others nor reckon upon promises not being kept," or he who is conscious beforehand of deceit, that is the true sage? (XIV, 33)

Another aspect of *jen* parallels what research has taught us about the trusting heart as well. The Chinese character for *jen* is the ideogram for that which is common in two men, suggesting that *jen* is a common denominator of humankind, an inborn seed-essence of humanity.

This idea was developed further by Mencius (371–289 B.C.E.), who was revered by the Chinese as the Second Sage, second only to Confucius. Mencius declared that human nature is basically good, that *jen* springs from human feelings that are innate and universal. In Mencius's view, man possesses an inborn vital element—*ch'i* (sometimes translated as "ether")—that comprises these innate feelings. If cultivated through education and proper upbringing, the *ch'i* is developed to the fullest extent, at which point the decree of Heaven and the nature of man become indistinguishable. As Mencius put it:

All the ten thousand living things are found within us. There is no greater joy than to look into our life and find this true. . . . He that goes to the bottom of his heart knows his own nature and knowing his own nature he knows Heaven.

For me, the Confucian idea that *jen* can be obtained by understanding one's own nature calls to mind research suggesting that certain biological characteristics of the nervous system—robust endorphin and calming-branch responses—present even in infants, may predispose one to the development of a more trusting attitude toward others.

TAOISM

Along with Confucianism, Taoism is the other major religio-philosophical tradition in Chinese life. Growing out of prehistorical origins, what we now know of Taoism is based largely on the preserved teachings of Lao-tzu (6th—5th century B.C.E.) and Chuang-tzu (4th—3rd century B.C.E.), the most widely known source being Lao-tzu's *Tao-te Ching*.

The aspect of Taoism that is most relevant to the trusting heart is the emphasis Taoism places on doing away with the distinction between the self and the world. Knowing that all beings are one, the Taoist pursues the ideal of *wu-wei*, a form of action in which there is no act, yet nothing is left undone. Since all beings and everything are fundamentally one, there is no need to oppose others. Clearly, this is in opposition to the purposes of what we have come to call the hostile heart, which does not trust others, is self-involved, and very concerned with "I," "me," and "mine." The Taoist holy man offers no resistance to any potential opponent, since "When you argue, there are some things you are failing to see. In the greatest Tao nothing is named; in the greatest disputation, nothing is said" (Chuang-tzu).

The doing away with focus on the self is highlighted

in Chuang-tzu's advice to those who want to know the Tao
(Way):

> Don't meditate, don't cogitate . . . : Follow no school,
> follow no way, and then you will attain the Tao; discard
> knowledge, forget distinctions, reach no-knowledge.
> [Those who speak about the Tao] are wholly wrong. For
> he who knows does not speak; he who speaks does not
> know.

CONCLUSIONS

It should be clear by now that within the world's
major religions are to be found teachings that appear remarkably similar to what research has taught us about the
nature of hostility, its bases, and its health consequences.

Throughout these religious traditions we find a preferred way of being, described as one wherein we are advised
to: look for the good in others, rather than the bad; treat
others well, just as we would like to be treated ourselves;
cease to be so concerned with our own selves, but direct our
attention and acts more toward other beings, even all cre-
ation. Moreover, as we have seen, many religious traditions
express the notion that those who follow the preferred way
will live longer, though merely achieving long life can
never be an adequate reason for following the better way.
Finally, we have seen in many traditions the idea that as
humans we contain something within us—whether described as "*ch'i*" or the "kingdom of God"—that somehow
motivates and enables us to follow the preferred way.

That the world religions have many teachings in common is not a new recognition. Aldous Huxley was one who
devoted much study and thought to the philosophical as-

pects of religion. Even he, after all his efforts to understand world religions, told an audience shortly before his death, "It is a little embarrassing that, after forty-five years of research and study, the best advice I can give to people is to be a little kinder to each other."

But what does it matter that the research on the trusting heart—showing that those who like others, who experience less anger, and who treat others kindly are more likely to live longer; or suggesting that there are biological characteristics of people that both make it more likely they will have a trusting heart *and* live longer—leads us to the same conclusions as the foregoing review of world religious teachings?

For me, it is simply enough to say that I find it very "interesting" that scientific research and religious strivings have pointed to such similar conclusions. Perhaps it will soften the attitudes of those who find little personal use for religion to know that science points to "truths" espoused by over two thousand years of religious tradition. And perhaps learning that such a wide range of humanity's religious thought points to emerging scientific truths also will calm those who feel threatened by science.

There are many ways of knowing. Jesus, the Jewish Fathers, Gautama, Confucius, Lao-tzu, all had ways of knowing that led them, somehow, to the realizations that informed their teachings. The scientific method is simply another way of "knowing" that has led to the insights described in this book about the health benefits of having a trusting heart.

Are the conclusions of science more valid because they agree in so many respects with the religious teachings? Should we have more confidence in the religious teachings because they are "supported" by objective scientific evidence? My preference would be to say that when different ways of knowing point to the same conclusion, I have more confidence in the truth of that conclusion—as well as in the two means used to reach it.

The best answer to these questions, however, might be expressed by this Buddhist saying, itself a question:

When a finger points out the moon in the night sky, which is more worthy of our attention, the finger, or the moon to which it points?

PART TWO

TOWARD A MORE TRUSTING HEART

EIGHT

BEFORE WE START

I know what you want.

You want me to tell you, in five simple, easy steps, how to have a more trusting heart and thus avoid—or even cure—a heart attack, cancer, or some other life-threatening illness. Perhaps something along the lines of "If you eat five grapefruits a day, you can eat all the steak and dessert you want every day and still lose five pounds per week!"

Would that it were so simple and easy. But it's not, and I would be misleading you if I suggested otherwise. Simple? Maybe. But easy? I'm afraid not. There is a large body of research showing that personality traits are very stable over time in the same individual. On a more personal level, I know it's not easy because I have tried to reduce my own cynicism, anger, and aggressive responding tendencies.

Despite my extensive understanding of how a cynical, mistrusting attitude toward others, anger, and aggressive treatment of others can place one at higher risk of serious health problems, I still find myself harboring nasty thoughts about the motives of slow people ahead of me in supermarket lines, of drivers who are still sitting there after the traffic light has changed to green, even of unseen folks on some other floor of the building when the elevator doesn't arrive fast enough to suit me. It doesn't take long, of course, before those nasty thoughts become feelings— feelings of anger at the dumb cluck who can't even read the sign that says "EXPRESS CHECKOUT—No more than 10 items." If I don't catch myself, I might even give that person a piece of my mind: "Excuse me, ma'am, [clipped tones] would you like to borrow my glasses so you can read the sign above this line?"

Even though I am as aware as anyone of the potential harm that can result from such thoughts, feelings, and behaviors, I still experience and even, on occasion, especially if I am tired or stressed out, express them. But not nearly as much as I used to; at an earlier point in my life I was much worse. If you don't believe me, ask my wife.

So it *is* possible to reduce our hostility, to become more trusting. I believe this not only because of my own experiences, but also because of some very important research conducted by Dr. Meyer Friedman. In this study, the Recurrent Coronary Prevention Project (RCPP), Dr. Friedman and his colleagues recruited 1,000 male heart attack victims—all Type A—to participate in a study evaluating various preventive approaches following a heart attack. Two-thirds of the men, about 650, were randomly assigned to a behavior-modification treatment program designed to reduce both the time urgency and free-floating hostility aspects of their Type A behavior; the other one-third, about 350 men, were assigned to a standard, state-of-the-art cardiac rehabilitation program.

After the treatment programs were completed, independent assessments showed the men in the behavior-modification group had decreased their Type A behavior (both time urgency and hostility) by a substantial degree. Those in the standard cardiac rehabilitation group had also decreased their Type A behavior, but to a far smaller extent. These results provided strong evidence that it is possible to reduce the time-urgency and hostility components of the Type A behavior pattern.

More important, there was a significant reduction in the rate of recurrent heart problems in the behavior-modification group. Subsequent follow-up of the men in the RCPP has also found reduced mortality rates in the behavior-modification group. So it is possible to change some aspects of Type A behavior, and, at least in men who had a heart attack, this change appears associated with a better prognosis.

These findings, suggesting that behavior changes *following* a heart attack may reduce the risk of having a second attack, provide some encouragement that reducing hostility should be beneficial in preventing a first heart attack. Indeed, it is in this area of *primary prevention*—avoiding the initial development of disease—that the greatest potential benefits are to be found.

We have marvelous medical technologies available for the fixing of sick hearts, and more are being developed and put into practice every day. No longer is major surgery— having your chest cut open so that surgeons can "bypass" clogged arteries—the only form of intervention available to prevent further damage in a heart whose blood supply is already compromised. With the aid of new types of catheters (small tubes that can be threaded through arteries back into the heart itself), cardiologists are now able to inflate a balloon at a site of arterial narrowing and relieve the blockage. On the way are even more advanced catheters with miniature lasers on the end that (like the "Roto-Rooter" plumbers use to unclog your drain) can clean out the arteriosclerotic plaques from your coronary arteries. And exciting new drug approaches are being developed, such as "tissue plasminogen activator" (TPA), that, if given in time, can dissolve clots in coronary arteries and stop a heart attack in progress before the heart muscle is damaged.

All of these developments are having a dramatic impact on the problems associated with coronary heart disease, and are probably, along with our efforts to reduce risk factors, major reasons for the decline in mortality rates due to coronary disease over the past ten years. Encouraging as these new treatments for existing coronary heart disease are, we must also keep in mind that, despite the improvements, heart attack is still the leading cause of death in the United States. Many of these deaths occur in middle-aged men who die suddenly, before they can be helped by the new approaches. And even among those who are helped, whose lives are saved by the new approaches, their heart muscle is still damaged, and their ability to lead a fully active life is often reduced.

As previously noted, it is easier to repair a small defect than it is to make major repairs later on. Primary prevention of disease—not just coronary heart disease, but cancer and other major forms of illness as well—in the long run will prove far more effective, far less costly, and far less disruptive than all the modern medical technological miracles we can devise to fix the heart or kill the cancer once disease is present and affecting organ function.

Yes, Dr. Friedman's study of the male heart attack victims showed it is possible, once heart disease is present, to improve your chances of avoiding further heart problems by reducing your feelings of hostility and time urgency. And there are many reports of patients with very serious diseases, even advanced cancers, who were able, often in association with intense practice of some mental disciplines, to achieve remissions and even apparent cures.

But we must be realistic. Once a disease process has advanced beyond a certain point, the biology of the disease itself alters the situation and takes on a life of its own. Even simple measures that might, if applied earlier, have *prevented* the disease from ever getting past the initial stages may no longer be effective once the disease has gained a foothold in the body.

I do not wish to be discouraging here. There is much that can be done by modern medicine once disease is present. Untold lives have already been saved or prolonged by such measures, and coming advances in medical research will lead to even greater hope for disease victims in the future.

And I do believe that the changes in attitudes, feelings, and behaviors that can be achieved by following the paths described in this book *may* be helpful once disease is present. They will certainly not be harmful, *unless* their use leads persons with serious illnesses to fail to take advantage of the help modern medicine has to offer.

Let me be very explicit here. If you or a loved one have heart disease, cancer, or some other serious illness, it is essential—first and foremost—that you be under the care of a physician who is able to bring to bear all the truly wondrous tools available from modern medicine, because these will enable him or her to ensure that you have the best possible chance of cure or at least of being able to live well with the disease. The biology of disease is a powerful force that alters the normal functioning of your entire body, and powerful tools are needed to change this biology for the better.

If you or a loved one has a serious disease and are under the ongoing care of a physician who is bringing to bear what medicine has to offer, then, by all means, try the approaches I suggest. But do not let your use of these techniques keep you from getting the best care medicine has to offer for your condition. These behavior-change techniques are not in opposition to standard medical practice in the treatment of disease. They may provide adjunctive help, but they are never a substitute for medical treatment when major disease is present.

What I am about to do, then, is provide you with some information you can use to develop a more trusting heart— knowledge and skills that will help to reduce your cynical thoughts, your angry feelings, and your aggressive behaviors.

Will these approaches cure cancer or mend wounded hearts? Probably not; I would rely more on modern medical science for those jobs. Will they increase your chances of cure or longer survival when added to modern medical techniques? I honestly don't know. I *think* it possible they might; and I am sure that they will not hurt, so long as their employment does not keep you from obtaining the best available medical care.

I cannot prove to you at present that having a more trusting heart will prevent you from developing a serious illness in the first place. But such proof is not required before we may conclude it is prudent to begin efforts to reduce hostility. For example, the association between some risk factors—high cholesterol and smoking—and disease was sufficient to lead doctors and health planners to advise the U.S. population to take steps to reduce their levels of those risk factors even before we had research results documenting that such reductions would indeed lead to reduced disease.

I believe the situation with hostility is similar. There is now considerable evidence that high levels of hostility identify a group that has unusually high mortality rates, particularly in the midlife years. This alone makes it wise, I believe, to begin steps to reduce hostility levels, even in the absence of definitive evidence that so doing will prevent disease. The case for taking such a course is made considerably stronger by Dr. Friedman's study showing actual reductions in coronary problems in men given training in how to reduce their hostility and time urgency. And finally, if for no other reason, it is worth the effort to reduce hostility and have a more trusting heart because to do so will make our lives more tranquil, will make us better spouses, parents, friends, and lovers.

When life-threatening diseases loom in our lives or the lives of those we love, it is impossible not to hope for a miracle. As I said, modern medicine *does* have "miracles" to offer those whose lives are threatened by heart disease, cancer, and other killing diseases. While a trusting heart may provide some benefit to those already stricken, I believe a far more realistic "miracle" to expect from making hearts more trusting will be heart attacks not suffered at all, cancers that never start—in other words, from disease prevented rather than from disease cured.

The task of becoming a more trusting heart can be undertaken at two levels. At the level of our families, there are things we can do to help our children grow up to have trusting hearts. At the level of the individual, there are three paths we can follow in trying to have a trusting heart. These paths are, the behavior-modification path, the religious path, and the medical path.

These paths are by no means mutually exclusive. One path, or even some parts of one path, may appeal more to some than to others; while for others a different path may be a more effective way to a trusting heart. That's fine. Read on, try out for yourself some of the techniques I suggest, and adopt the mix of the paths that works best for you.

NINE

LET'S HAVE MORE TRUSTING CHILDREN

The bumper sticker reads, "Have you hugged your kid today?" If, as a society, we can address this question positively—not just in terms of "a hug," but with respect to its broader implications for how we regard and treat our children—it might do more, over time, to reduce hostility and increase the proportion of trusting hearts in our population than all other measures combined.

Let me encourage you to review the earlier section, referring to hostility as a learned phenomenon and the role of nurture. There we learned that, even from the first moments of life, the human infant is capable of learning to look for nurturing care, and of experiencing distress—perhaps the forerunner of mistrust—when learned expectations are not met. We learned that loving touch may be necessary for growth, even for life itself. We learned that in rats very early experiences can lead to changes in the

brain that render the adult animal less reactive (more resistant) to stress—and that those findings may have implications for humans. And we learned that certain types of
family environments appear more likely to produce hostile,
angry children than others.

These things all teach us that how we treat and care
for our children, even our newborn children, may exert
profound effects on their growth and development, as well
as how they come to view the world and the people in it.

The differences between American and Japanese
child-rearing practices provided a case in point. In contrast
to Western attitudes and practices, in Japan the child is
regarded as basically good and free from bad or evil intentions; frequent close physical contact between mother and
child is the norm. It is difficult to be sure of cause-and-effect
relationships in such matters, but it is likewise hard to
ignore the perhaps culturally determined connection between such child-rearing practices and the presence in the
normal adult Japanese personality of *amae,* the expectation
that others will behave benevolently toward one. The preliminary evidence of lower hostility scale scores among
Japanese may be the direct result of these child-rearing
practices.

Of course, there are many other characteristics besides
amae that are common to the Japanese personality. It is
striking, however, that *amae* is so much the opposite of the
cynicism aspect of hostility, *and* that it seems so directly
rooted in how the Japanese regard and treat their children.
If, as Dr. Friedman believes, the absence of "unconditional
love, affection, and encouragement" from one or both parents is one of the prime stimuli toward Type A behavior,
might not the Japanese model provide us with at least one
example of how the presence of these experiences can lead
to high levels of interpersonal trust?

I believe so, and offer the following recommendations
as a means of treating our children in ways that will in-

crease the likelihood that, as adults, they will have trusting hearts.

Rather than assuming our children will behave badly if given the chance, let us strive to think of our children as inherently good, wonderful, clever, and full of delight, and act accordingly. Easier said than done, of course, but it helps to consider *why* we are trying to do it—to provide our children with a world view that will enable them to grow up to lead healthier, longer, and more satisfying lives.

Hopefully, such attitudes will modify our family environments enough to be conducive to the production of less hostile, less angry children.

From the very beginning, it is important to expose our newborn children to frequent, loving touch. Rather than only hovering nearby, like the American mothers Dr. Caudill observed in his studies of American and Japanese parenting practices, let us emulate the Japanese mother and pick up the baby and comfort it with loving human contact as soon as it starts to cry. Even though it runs counter to maternal instincts, pediatricians have been known to tell new mothers to "Go ahead and let your baby cry. It's good exercise for the lungs." Don't even ask for such advice, and if it is given, ignore it. When the baby cries, pick it up and love it. And remember, fathers can provide such loving touch too.

What if this approach doesn't quiet the baby? What if your baby is one of those whose nervous system is so irritable he or she doesn't respond to such comforting and continues to cry and squirm? It is true that some babies *are* harder to comfort than others; they don't even like to suckle long at the breast, and even start to wriggle if held overlong. Perhaps they are this way because, as we speculated earlier, their brain opioid responses are deficient, or their autonomic nervous system's calming branch doesn't kick in soon enough to quiet the emergency branch's commotion. I would say go ahead and keep trying with such children. Don't give up, but continue to pick them up when they cry and try your best to comfort them with loving touch and words (even if they don't understand the content of the words, the tone will convey your meaning). Here's why I think it will work.

Our first "child" was a beautiful black cat named Ubiquity, whom we adopted in the second winter we were married, when she was about nine months old. Since I was in medical school and my wife, Virginia, was teaching school, we had little time to devote to Ubiquity, and she remained quite wild, refusing to "cuddle up" to us. When the summer came, we rented a house on the Connecticut shore, and every day while I was back in town at the medical center doing a summer research fellowship, Virginia would spend a good part of the day holding and stroking Ubiquity, telling her what a wonderful, beautiful cat she was. At first Ubiquity didn't like it and would try to run away, but Virginia persisted, chasing her down and showering the frightened cat with loving touch and words. By the end of the summer, Ubiquity responded to this attention, and she returned the love she had received many times over before she died at the ripe old age of 15.

I believe babies are just as smart as cats. Therefore, don't give up if your baby is one of those irritable squirmers. Persist with loving touch and words and I bet that, even if it takes all summer, you'll never regret that you did. Harvard's Dr. Kagan believes that, even though innate biological factors contribute much to the shy, inhibited temperament, how a child is treated, the kind of environment he or she experiences, can modulate how much the biological predisposition to shyness is expressed. Just because a trait is "genetic" doesn't mean we can't change or channel it in healthier directions.

Research has shown warm human contact to be necessary not only for growth but to life itself. It should also help the infant to establish a sense of basic trust in the goodness of the world and the people in it.

As our children grow, we must continue to think of them as basically good (even say, "My kid is basically good," over to yourself five times if you have to whenever you find yourself harboring thoughts to the contrary). We should be on the lookout for instances when their behavior is consistent with this inner goodness and lavish them with praise for such behaviors. In other words, catch them doing something good and reward them.

Never criticize them or ask if they can do better when they are being good. Avoid physical punishment; actually, it is a good idea to avoid all kinds of punishment if you can. Rather than calling attention to their misbehavior, you might even ignore them, as long as no harm or injury is risked. I advise this because, while positive reinforcement—reward—is pretty straightforward in its consequences ("rewarded behaviors" increase in frequency), negative reinforcement—punishment—is much trickier. Sometimes what we think of as punishment may be perceived by our child as actually rewarding, because it is, at least, some form of attention. Of course, this is particularly likely to happen when they learn that doing good things is not effective in getting our attention.

It stands to reason that treating our children as we ourselves would like to be treated is a logical extension of our discussion. But in addition, our goal is to help them grow up to be more trusting, less angry, and to treat others kindly. Thus, when they are exhibiting any of these behaviors, praise them, tell them what great kids they are. Conversely, when they act up, as all kids will, simply ignore them, as long as there is no risk of harm or injury.

There is not sufficient room to provide you here with a complete treatise on how to raise less hostile, more trusting children. But there are certainly a few guidelines I might mention, for each of the three goals of more trust, less anger, and more kindness. For more detailed, in-depth guidance, you might read *Parent Effectiveness Training*.

To encourage more trust, try to reward your child's statements that indicate friendliness: In response to "It's fun to play with Sally," you might say, "It's great that you have friends you like to be with." Try to reward expressions of empathy on your child's part for the distress of others. Encourage empathy by modeling it for your child, that is, be openly empathetic yourself. And when your child expresses the opposite of these qualities, say nothing; look off into the distance for a few seconds, and then change the subject.

Look for opportunities to praise your child when he is expressing happiness and joy in words or facial expressions—"What a handsome boy you are when you smile like that!" When he is expressing anger that is not really justified, from a sour face to a falling-down temper tantrum, try to ignore it. Remember that ignoring it is not the same as punishing it; ignoring it simply says to your child that there is not going to be any response from Mom or Dad—or Grandmom or Granddad—for this. Punishing it can say this is a way to get some extra attention from Mom or Dad, or it's dangerous to be angry and I'd better keep my feelings to myself.

A good strategy when your child is angry is to use the situation to teach empathy—for example, by encouraging him or her to think about the reasons behind another child's bad behavior. And if your child's anger is clearly justified by what he or she is responding to, by all means say something like, "Well, I can certainly see how that would be upsetting to you." By doing this, you are modeling empathy for your child in the most effective way possible, by empathizing with his or her legitimate feelings.

To encourage kind and considerate treatment of others, "catch" your child treating someone else well and administer a hefty dose of praise. And don't forget to model this behavior by treating others well yourself. Indeed, remember that the more children are exposed to aggression in the course of growing up—physical punishment or violence toward them by their parents, television portrayals of aggression, and the like—the more likely they are later to be aggressive themselves.

I can hear you thinking, If I want my kid to be more trusting, less angry, and kinder to others, I'm going to have to be that way myself!

How right you are. It's truly amazing how observant and perceptive kids are. No matter what we may be saying—all those expressions of positive reinforcement alluded to above—if inside we really don't mean it, if at the same time we're saying "Poor Mrs. Johnson . . ." we have an expression of disgust on our face, then our children will know what we really feel. And *that* will be what they copy; that will more likely be the aspect of our behavior they model than the superficial content of what we said. Remember, emotions expressed on our faces are very powerful biological signals.

So the best way to have trusting, less angry, kinder kids is to be that way ourselves. This is a double benefit for the parent, since he'll be encouraging a trusting heart in *himself* as well as in his child. Let's now go on to how you can move toward this goal.

TEN

IS YOURS
A HOSTILE HEART?

I t has always been in order to have a more trusting heart; this is what the world's religions have taught for well over two thousand years. Now, I believe for the first time, there is another reason: scientific evidence showing that trusting hearts live longer, healthier lives.

In terms of the medical model, of course, diagnosis comes before treatment. Before you decide to undertake steps toward a more trusting heart yourself, you need to determine whether yours is a hostile heart and hence in need of change. How can you be sure you have those cynical, angry, and aggressive aspects of hostility that are predicting all those health problems?

To enable you to answer this question, I shall describe in a fairly realistic way the kinds of thoughts, feelings, and actions that characterize the typical person with a hostile heart, the kind of person who should be better off with a more trusting heart. If, as you read these descriptions you find yourself nodding in recognition, then read on, for in later chapters I shall outline the paths you might follow toward a more trusting heart. If the descriptions fit someone you care about, and if you feel comfortable sharing this impression with him or her, please do so.

You'll recall that the three aspects of hostility that appear to be particularly toxic are: (1) cynical beliefs that others are inherently bad, selfish, mean, and not to be trusted; (2) frequent angry feelings when these negative expectations are frequently fulfilled; and (3) the overt expression of these angry feelings in aggressive acts directed toward others.

Let me emphasize very strongly that what I will describe below is not some form of mental illness, craziness, or criminal tendency. These experiences all fall within the *normal* range of human psychology. If you recognize yourself in what follows, don't suppose you must be ready for jail or a mental hospital; what you are ready for is simply the rest of this book.

Indeed, there are many famous, successful, and even admired figures who fit these descriptions quite well. In his book *Treating Type A and Your Heart,* Dr. Friedman notes that President Lyndon B. Johnson displayed many of the characteristics typical of time urgency and free-floating hostility.

Another famous person whose hostility was quite well documented is William S. Gilbert of the Gilbert and Sullivan team that wrote so many well-loved operettas. As described by Israel Shenker in *Smithsonian* magazine, Gilbert was "prickly, disputatious, dictatorial, by nature choleric, by temperament unforgiving." Gilbert was forever getting in rows with cabmen who didn't deliver service up to his standards, and he was frequently involved in lawsuits directed toward those he felt had wronged him. Around the border of a glowering pen-and-ink self-portrait, Gilbert wrote the following antisocial statements, each one signed. "I hate my fellow-man." "I like pinching little babies." "I am an ill-tempered pig, and I glory in it." "Everybody is an Ass." "I love to bully."

So you are in quite good company (well, in some ways!) if the following descriptions fit you. One additional note of interest about Gilbert: he was not burdened by guilt at his bad behavior; he *did* glory in it. Not some neurotic weakling, he saw his attitudes and behavior as quite justified, proper, and appropriate. It is likely that you may feel the same way, that your poor opinions of others are quite justified by their atrocious behavior, and that they more than deserve it when you soundly blast them. Unfortunately, for our purposes, whether you are justified or not is beside the point. Such an attitude only hinders your efforts to become a more trusting heart. If you find your righteous indignation is getting the upper hand in your life and exploding with some frequency in your relationships with others, it's important for you to be aware of your feelings, to examine your indignation a bit more closely. Is it perhaps less justified than your first reaction might indicate?

A cynical mistrust of others is the driving force behind hostility; it makes us vigilant to their faults. Expecting that others will mistreat us, we are on the lookout for their bad behavior—and we can usually find it. This generates the frequent anger to which the hostile person is prone, and that anger, combined with a lack of empathy for others—a natural consequence of the poor opinion we hold of others in general—leads us to express our hostility overtly, in the form of aggressive acts toward others.

Probably the most characteristic attitude of the person with high levels of cynical mistrust is his suspicion of the motives of people he doesn't even know. If you have pushed the elevator button and the elevator stops two floors above for a bit longer than normal, do you soon begin to think, "How inconsiderate! You'd think if people wanted to carry on a conversation, they'd get off the elevator so the rest of us could get to where we're going!" You cannot see the people two floors above you, you cannot hear them (even if, as your cynicism often leads you to do, you press your ear to the elevator door to confirm your suspicions), and you have no earthly way of knowing what is really holding up the elevator. Yet, in the span of a few seconds your cynical mistrust has led you to draw hostile conclusions about the unseen people in the elevator, their selfish motives and inconsiderate behavior—and you're driving yourself to distraction.

It is a simple matter to make up similar scenarios—involving the express checkout line at the supermarket described earlier, for example, or the driver of the car ahead of you who waits too long after the traffic light turns green to start off, or you may find yourself disparaging fat people, "who can't even take the trouble to lose enough weight to look decent in public." If your own thoughts in these situations are similar to those I described, you likely have too much of the cynical-mistrust aspect of hostility. If you can easily think of several other situations in your daily life that frequently stimulate such reactions in you, then for sure you do. When I give talks to lay audiences—ranging from heart patients to healthy advertising executives—I never get too far into the descriptions of these situations that tweak our cynicism nerve before several members of the audience start to laugh, either at the remembrance of the many times they got hot under the collar in those ways, or at their susceptible table-mates. Many of us have this cynical mistrust.

It is far less funny, however, when, instead of unseen strangers, these thoughts are directed at our loved ones—for example, at the wife who can't cook the spaghetti without its sticking together because she doesn't stir it enough. Or at the child whose sin was to spill food at the table. Or at the husband who manages to botch every repair job he attempts around the house.

Sound familiar? Is it easy for you to think of several similar examples? If so, you can be sure your level of cynical mistrust is above average, probably in the range that puts you in a higher risk group for health problems. Note carefully: I am not saying it means that you personally are headed straight for a heart attack; rather, it means that this level of hostility places you in a *group* whose risk of serious health problems is higher than that of groups without this particular characteristic. Is this a group you want to stay with?

Equally bad, cynical mistrust at this level has effects on those around you that are definitely undesirable. Even if you don't utter a word in these situations, the anger, or the disgust you feel, is written on your face for all to see. The message you give to your husband, wife, or child with such facial expressions is that they are incompetent, that you believe they did it on purpose, and that they are in danger of being rejected by you. Not a very nice message to be sending, is it? Probably not the one you really intend, either.

What's worse still, these kinds of communications have effects on the behaviors of others, *causing them to behave in ways that meet our expectations, to fulfill our cynical prophecies.* It's relatively harmless when the objects of our mistrust are strangers we are unlikely to see again. It is quite another proposition when it is our spouse and children whom we are influencing with our cynical mistrust every day, day after day after day. No wonder family resemblances in hostility scale scores have been found!

And what about the people whose cynicism is so high that anger is experienced too often? If the thoughts I described earlier are the "words" of hostility, the emotions, the intense feelings of irritation, rage, frustration, of wanting to lash out at the source of these feelings—in a word, *anger*—are the "music" of hostility.

You can tell when the thoughts indicative of cynical mistrust are generating anger in you not only by recognizing the emotions just described, but also by the increasing physical symptoms of the fight-or-flight response described earlier. These symptoms, most of which stem from the effects of the outpouring of adrenaline (epinephrine), include a change in your voice to a higher pitch (adrenaline tightens your vocal cords), an increase in the rate and depth of your breathing, awareness that your heart is racing and beating harder—"pounding"—in your chest, a sensation of tightness in the muscles of your arms and legs, and a general feeling of being "charged up," ready for intense action. In the laboratory it is possible to induce such a physical reaction in people with high levels of hostility, as for example, in Dr. Ed Suarez's harassment experiment (see page 105). Most people do not experience the emotions or physical symptoms of the fight-or-flight reaction as pleasant; for most of us they are quite distressing.

If you frequently experience these feelings in situations like those described earlier, it is likely that your anger quotient is too high, so high that it means you belong to the group at increased risk of developing serious health problems in the future. Indeed, it is most likely the biological consequences of the hormones—epinephrine, norepinephrine, and cortisol—poured out during these anger episodes that lead over time to disease.

It is also possible that less-than-efficient blunting of these hormonal effects by your calming branch could be part of the biological pathway to disease. By leaving you at the continuing mercy of the unpleasant effects of adrenaline on your body, your weak calming branch could also be responsible in part for your feeling a need to do something "extra" to reduce these distressing feelings.

This need is the source of the third toxic aspect of hostility that we must discuss: the aggressive behaviors that result when the pressure from our cynical thoughts and anger becomes too much to bear without doing something, usually some kind of aggressive act directed toward the person who gets our cynical thoughts going in the first place.

Sometimes this is expressed as an outburst of rage, wherein we might literally scream at the person stimulating our anger. If, for example, you have *ever* yelled at a child for accidentally spilling some food or drink on the floor (when you weren't already under a lot of stress for other legitimate reasons), or if you have often upbraided your wife or husband for making a mess of some job in or around the house, then it is likely that the level of your aggressive response is high enough to need your attention.

Over time, it sadly becomes easier for the hostile heart to express anger toward family members or friends—familiarity breeds contempt. Most people manage to bridle their anger in the company of complete strangers, however. Have you, on the other hand, often been known to express your irritation to someone you never saw before two minutes ago? This can take the form of addressing that person, ranging from the mild—"I believe you have too many items in your basket for this EXPRESS CHECKOUT line"—all the way up to the not-so-mild—"Hey, you can't go through this line with that many items!" It can take the form of turning around to the person behind you, pointing to the sign above the line, and grimacing. It can take the form of yelling at your child to hurry up when he actually has plenty of time to make it to school. It can take the form of putting your car's headlights on bright to get back at someone who kept his brights on when he was behind you. The critical thing here is that you go beyond the cynical thoughts and angry feelings to the point of performing some *act*.

At this point, you may be muttering to yourself, "The only people who don't fit his descriptions are either wimps or dead!" You may be justified in having such a concern, so let me spell out in a bit more detail what kinds of acts are really aggressive. The first clue that your behavior in a given situation is hostile can be gleaned from your answer to the question "What is my purpose in doing this?" If at least part of your purpose is to *punish* the other person, to make him or her feel bad for what he or she has done, then you are guilty as charged—even if another purpose is to achieve some reasonable goal of your own. If a sense of "righteous indignation" can be said fairly to describe your state of mind as you say what you say, or do what you do, it is highly likely that your intention is at least in part hostile. Another clue that you are too aggressive is the frequency of your hostile acts: You nearly always honk after waiting a few seconds for the car ahead to move out; you always say something when caught in a slow-moving line.

But what about those times, you say, when the other person really *is* being bad, selfish, inconsiderate—for example, actually trying to butt ahead in line or assaulting you with a gratuitous insult? What about those times when your anger and some aggressive responses really are justified? Well, I would be the first to admit that there certainly are situations in daily life when others do behave selfishly, in ways that end up in your being unfairly mistreated. After all, I have just been telling you that a hostile heart is the norm for many of us. When such folks are doing their number on the world, sooner or later, they could be doing it on you.

So what about these situations, when your righteous indignation, anger, and lashing out are really justified— that is, not simply an outgrowth of your own cynical world view? I cannot prove it beyond a shadow of a doubt, but I believe that in over 90 percent of these situations your indignation, anger, and aggressive behavior are going to do you more harm than the thoughtless creature whose behavior stimulated them in you. So what if your feelings and behavior are "justified"? It's *your* arteries, *your* heart, *your* immune system, *your* muscles that are going to be bombarded by too much adrenaline, cortisol, and other stress hormones. You want to feel angry? You want to let that inconsiderate numbskull have a piece of your mind? Go ahead, but just remember, it's *your* body that may someday pay the price for it, not his. I would say the bottom line is, are your anger and aggressive response really going to accomplish any useful purpose right now?

Before you flip out completely, let me acknowledge this: There are times when you really must act, *not* to punish or get even with the other person who is mistreating you, but simply because his or her behavior is preventing, or might prevent, you from reaching some important goal. Let's say you are in that infamous Express Checkout Line again, but now, instead of having no real deadline, no fixed time by which you have to be out of the store, home with supper fixed, or on your way to an evening meeting in only thirty minutes—let's say this time you really *do* need to hurry for a perfectly legitimate purpose. And there ahead of you is this other person with twenty items, twice the limit. Should you simply stand there and stew, as perhaps you have inferred I was suggesting earlier?

The answer is no. I am getting a bit ahead of things here—into the behavior-modification path—but it is important to point out here that being *assertive* is not the same thing as being aggressive. If you say to the person ahead of you in line, in as calm a voice as you can muster, "Excuse me, but I see you have several items in your basket; I have many fewer in mine, but, more important, I really do have an important meeting to get to and need to get through this line as fast as possible. Could I impose upon you to let me go ahead? I would really appreciate it!" you are not being aggressive, you are simply informing him that you have a legitimate need not to be held up in the designated Express Line. Asking, in a polite way, for something you really need is being assertive, not aggressive. I must emphasize the "in a polite way," for unless you are careful, angry feelings will show in your tone of voice and on your face and stimulate the other person, no matter how polite the *content* of your words, to respond in kind.

To return to the larger point here: if you have those angry feelings and act hostilely (say something to the other person, beep the horn; by now you know what I mean) even when the other person is not *really* being selfish or mean (maybe it's someone who lost his glasses and whose eyesight is so poor he can't make out the permitted number of items), then you surely have a heart that is hostile enough to consider changing. If you experience these feelings and behave thus "only" when the other person's behavior justifies them, I would say you still have a problem, a smaller problem perhaps, but still a problem, for it will be your body that pays the price if you have the misfortune to be exposed to such people with any frequency.

Let's conclude with a quiz. Since you the reader are just one person, the results cannot be as scientific as they are when we are talking about large groups of people. (Recall the example of the physicist who can predict what large groups of electrons are going to do with exquisite accuracy, but whose predictions falter when the object is a single electron.) Nevertheless, you do need some more specific indication, beyond the descriptions just given, to determine if you belong to a group of people whose hostility places them at risk of health problems down the road.

Keeping the preceding descriptions in mind, answer the following questions by circling (or simply noting in your mind) the answer that best describes you.

1. When family members or even persons I don't know do things (or fail to do things) that hold me up or prevent me from doing something I wish to do, I begin to think that they are selfish, mean, inconsiderate, and the like:

NEVER   SOMETIMES   OFTEN   ALWAYS

2. When strangers, friends, or members of my family do things that seem incompetent, messy, selfish, or inconsiderate, I quickly experience feelings of frustration, anger,

irritation, and even rage; at the same time I become aware of these feelings, I notice unpleasant bodily sensations, like trouble getting enough breath, my heart pounding rapidly in my chest, my palms sweating, and the like:

NEVER   SOMETIMES   OFTEN   ALWAYS

3. When I have the thoughts, feelings, and bodily sensations just described, I am very likely to express my feelings in some way—whether by words, gestures, tone of voice, or facial expressions—to the other person or persons who I see as responsible for my unpleasant thoughts and feelings:

NEVER   SOMETIMES   OFTEN   ALWAYS

If you answer OFTEN or ALWAYS to at least two of the above, then it is very likely that your hostility level places you in a group that is at higher risk of health problems. Even if you did not answer in this way, but if the scenarios I described earlier struck a responsive chord in you, I would still advise you to read on as we next examine the three paths to a more trusting heart.

ELEVEN

THE BEHAVIOR-MODIFICATION PATH: TWELVE STEPS TO A TRUSTING HEART

To have a more trusting heart is not easy; it requires you to work toward three separate but related goals:

First, reduce your cynical mistrust of the motives of others.

Second, reduce the frequency and intensity with which you experience negative emotions of anger, irritation, frustration, rage, and the like.

And *third,* rather than behaving aggressively toward others, learn to treat others with kindness and consideration, and develop your positive assertiveness skills for use in those unavoidable situations that will crop up.

In other words, to have a more trusting heart, you will need to change your thoughts, your feelings, and your actions. This is the sort of approach that Dr. Meyer Friedman and his associates took to reduce Type A behavior in the Recurrent Coronary Prevention Project. As we now know, it may not be necessary to concentrate so much on reducing time urgency as it is to reduce hostility. Granted, it is often a situation involving loss of time that elicits the thoughts, feelings, and actions of the hostile heart; but it is not the time urgency per se that does the harm so much as it is the hostile person's reaction to it. Many situations besides those that involve potential loss of time, however, stir up the hostile person's anger: for example, the spilled milk mentioned earlier, our thoughts of the "lazy poor" who are unwilling to work, even all the "crooked" politicians we regard as out for everything they can get. Rightly or wrongly, we can't change the world; but we can change our thoughts about the world.

How *does* one change thoughts? How do you stop those cynical thoughts I described earlier? How do you keep from declaring to yourself or others, "How inconsiderate! You'd think whoever's holding the elevator two floors up would know others need to move!" or "Why can't she learn how to cook spaghetti without allowing it to stick into a congealed mess? After all the times I've told her I can't stand it when it sticks together like that, you'd think she'd learn!"

The first step on this path is to have a reason for changing your hypercritical thoughts; in other words, to have *motivation*. Since you have already diagnosed yourself as having too much cynical mistrust, and learned that this may place you at higher risk of serious health problems, motivation shouldn't be too much of a problem at this point. You have other reasons for wanting to change, too, of course: to be a better parent, spouse, or friend. But it doesn't hurt to have the additional motivation that such a change may be as good for your health as it is for your relationships. I've devised the following twelve-step program you can follow to do just that: to change from a hostile to a trusting heart.

STEP ONE: MONITOR YOUR CYNICAL THOUGHTS

With a powerful reason to change these thoughts and a knowledge of the general character of the thoughts that need changing, you are in position to take the first step—monitoring your thoughts as you go through each day, to learn more about the frequency of and kinds of situations that trigger your cynical thoughts.

To begin, do this: Carry around with you a little pocket notebook. This is your hostility log. Whenever you realize you are thinking cynical thoughts, make an entry—later, if you are around other people, but don't put it off and forget it—in your Logbook. Every entry should include the time and place, who did what to stimulate the cynical thoughts (whether a specific person, such as the one you think is holding the elevator, or a general group, such as politicians or everybody in a given country, like Iran or the Soviet Union), the actual thought content that went through your head, the emotions you felt, and any action you took.

Your record keeping is meant to go beyond focusing on cynical thoughts; it should record angry feelings and aggressive acts as well. Since these aspects of hostility are also forms of behavior you will want to change (we'll get to how in a bit), you will need to monitor them too. A typical page from your hostility log might look something like this:

WHEN: Tues., 1/22/89, 1:15 P.M.

WHERE: In car, driving back from lunch to office

WHO: Young man, prob. a teenager, in a Ford Mustang

WHAT: Raced past me, cut in front of me, then slowed down for a right turn

THOUGHTS: Damn teenage drivers! Got to show how macho he is by cutting me off and then dawdles because *he* decides to turn!

FEELINGS: Annoyance, irritation, urge to kill

ACTIONS: Laid on the horn as I went by his turning car, gave him a mean look

As you begin to keep your hostility log, you will learn more than you ever knew about the frequency and kinds of situations that stir you up. The actual practice of keeping the log will sharpen your ability to recognize your cynical thoughts, angry feelings, and aggressive behaviors—and eventually to arrest them before they get started.

You must review your hostility log at the end of each week. It's important. Look for common themes in the situations that stir your hostility and write them down as a summary. You may be surprised at how often your hostility is aroused by what are really trivial events.

If you also begin to find yourself feeling somewhat guilty, if not downright ashamed, at how unimportant some of the situations were that you have down in the log, then you are already on the way to significant change. You have begun to realize how unrealistic some of your thoughts actually were. "That teenager wasn't trying to cut me off—heck, he was in a hurry and probably didn't realize how close his turn was." "Who knows why the elevator didn't come? For all I know, it could have been some handicapped person who needed extra time to get out."

Even when the thoughts may have been realistic—when the elevator finally arrives, two teenage girls are giggling about "the crazy things those boys keep saying"—the process of simply keeping the log and noting the situations, will likely lead you to conclude in many instances that it was still not worth getting angry over. After all, in that particular situation you were in no rush to get anywhere, you were simply waiting for the elevator on your way to run some minor errand with no particular deadline; and when you think about it a bit, those girls were certainly not trying to inconvenience anyone.

In fact, as you go over your hostility log, you are likely to realize that many, perhaps most, of the entries represent situations in which your own cynical mistrust was the major cause of the emotional reaction and the unpleasant behavior that resulted. This is a good start toward developing a trusting heart, but it probably won't be enough: Simple awareness of your hostility, and a rational understanding of its source, will take you partway toward a more trusting heart. But, like learning to hit a good backhand in tennis, it helps to have a few practice techniques to improve your trusting game as well. Hence, I've developed more steps to aid you in that difficult process.

STEP TWO: CONFESSION IS GOOD FOR THE SOUL

Remember all those TV ads where some famous person says, "Hello, I'm _____, and I'm a recovering alcoholic"? As Alcoholics Anonymous has learned through long experience, the open acknowledgment that we have a problem, want to do something about it, and actively seek the support of important people in our lives to do so can play a major role in our ultimate success. Therefore, let your spouse, or a close friend, know that you have recognized that you have a problem with too much hostility, and that you hope he or she will be supportive of your efforts to change.

This step offers several immediate benefits. Besides the important public step of going on record saying you have a problem, your acknowledgment is in a very real sense an act of trust directed toward the other person. To trust others enough to tell them about your hostility problem and ask for their support in coping with it can give you important "on the job" practice in trusting others.

If the other person is able to be supportive and help you in your efforts, you will in essence be rewarded for being more trusting. According to learning theory, behaviors that are rewarded are more likely to be repeated in the future. And, since it is likely that anyone you ask for such support will respond positively, this step can help reassure you that it is "safe" to trust others enough to ask for their help.

By now, you have acknowledged your problem and sought help in dealing with it, and you have improved your ability—by keeping a hostility log—to recognize those cynical thoughts. You are ready then for the next steps: some practical exercises to stop those thoughts altogether.

STEP THREE: STOP THOSE THOUGHTS!

How do you stop them? First of all, simply *tell them to stop.* Seriously—a well-known behavior-modification technique that has proven effective in helping patients who obsessively ruminate on the same thought all day long is known, simply, as "thought stopping." Here is how it works.

By keeping a hostility log, you have been improving your ability to recognize earlier and earlier in the hostility process when your cynical thoughts are gathering steam. Instead of realizing only *after* you are in a rage and your heart is pounding that you had been having nasty thoughts about that slow person ahead of you in the bank line, *now* you are becoming aware of those thoughts well before the hostility sequence progresses to anger and aggression.

As soon as you realize you are having the cynical thoughts, yell as loudly as you can (though silently to yourself), *"STOP!"* Interestingly enough, those thoughts *will* actually stop, and, if you are lucky, the anger, too, will be cut short before it gets started. If the thoughts start when you are alone, in response to something on the nightly TV news that incites your ire perhaps, by all means go ahead and yell out loud, at the top of your lungs, *"STOP!"*

STEP FOUR: REASON WITH YOURSELF

That sounds a bit artificial, silly even, you say? Okay, since you are a rational being, go ahead and try to reason with yourself—another perfectly good strategy. As the cynical thoughts begin there in the bank line, begin a silent conversation with yourself that goes something like this:

> All right, you suspicious person, you, here you go again, laying all these nefarious intentions on that harmless little old lady. Lighten up! You know darn well she didn't get out of bed this morning saying to herself, "By Jiminy, old _____ [here substitute your name] has gotta deposit that check down at the bank today. I'll just follow him down there, jump ahead of him in line, and really take forever; I won't even have a pen to fill out *my* deposit slip in the line. Hot dog! I can't wait to see him burn when I get there ahead of him in line."

This really might work, strictly on a rational basis. After all, you *know* that little old lady really didn't arise this morning with the main goal in her life being to get your goat. Even if it isn't the whole solution, the rational approach is worth the help it can offer.

STEP FIVE: PUT YOURSELF IN THE OTHER PERSON'S SHOES

You were accomplishing something else with your monologue: a feeling of empathy. When you put yourself in the other person's shoes in a joking way, imagining that the woman planned her day around irritating you, you could not avoid seeing how ridiculous your suspicions about her motives actually were. You might also gain the same sense of perspective in another way—by trying to understand others' behavior from *their* viewpoint; in most cases, you will find your anger slipping away. Empathy and anger are incompatible.

A more concrete way to increase your capacity for empathy is to engage regularly in altruistic, helping activities. You might want to become active in organizations that consider helping others a major purpose. The social outreach programs of your church or temple provide an excellent opportunity for this kind of activity. Other activities of this sort include recording for the blind, teaching reading to the illiterate, volunteering in your community's soup kitchen, helping to provide housing for the homeless. Every community has numerous associations organized around such goals. One national organization with local affiliates is Habitat for Humanity, which acquires land and builds houses for poor people, and which Jimmy and Rosalynn Carter have actively supported with their time and talents. I believe you will find it hard to suppress your empathic impulses if you regularly engage in altruistic behavior. Besides, such volunteer activities are likely to help you feel good, both physically and emotionally.

STEP SIX: LEARN TO LAUGH AT YOURSELF

Notice that you were doing something else in the conversation you were having with yourself just now: You were actually laughing at yourself. You were making fun of your own suspicious nature, and I would be surprised if you weren't actually beginning to get just the trace of a smile on your face as you went through the patently silly scenario of this little old lady planning her day around aggravating you.

Here, then, is another strategy you can use to deflect your cynical mistrust and defuse your anger: *humor.* I am sure many readers of this book have at least heard the story of how Norman Cousins conquered his serious illness by laughing through the day at old Marx Brothers movies. Whatever the truth of that matter, and whatever may be the actual biological effects of a belly laugh, it is almost impossible to stay angry when you are laughing, particularly when you are really and truly laughing at yourself, at your own foibles—consider it sort of the ultimate "in joke." (Let me remind you that what is essential is to be able to laugh at *yourself;* if you are laughing at the expense of others, you are really only displaying your cynicism in the form of ridicule.) If you can begin to make light fun of your cynical thoughts, you are well on your way to having a more trusting heart.

But let's say you have tried all of these six strategies, and, though you are somewhat better, you still find yourself harboring nasty thoughts about the people who impinge upon you, your anger still grows and grows, and, even though by now you really do know how important it is not to, you still, on occasion, really blast someone.

STEP SEVEN: LEARN TO RELAX

If you can't arrest your cynical thoughts by "thought stopping," by reasoning with yourself, or even by laughing at yourself, then it may be time for you to call upon a powerful technique that has been used for centuries to gain control over one's thoughts: meditation. As described in Dr. Herbert Benson's pioneering book, *The Relaxation Response,* meditation is perhaps the most effective means of emptying one's mind of all thoughts.

But to become proficient enough in this technique to be able to call upon it at will, you'll need to practice it regularly in private first, and at times when you aren't even "stressed out."

Here is what you do: Sit quietly and upright in a comfortable chair (but not a recliner; after all, your goal is not to go to sleep). Let your chin rest comfortably on your chest, your arms in your lap. Close your eyes. Next, begin to pay attention to your breathing. Simply *notice* when you breathe in and when you breathe out. Every time you inhale and every time you exhale, notice it and pay attention to the sensations of air flowing across the membranes in your nose and mouth, the feeling of your lungs filling with and expelling with air.

After you have done this for a few breaths, begin to repeat silently to yourself a single word every time you breathe out. The word you choose doesn't have to mean anything in particular. It can be a nonsense word you make up, or simply the number "one." On the other hand, it might be worth trying a word that conjures up the emotion you are trying to evoke with this strategy. Thus, you might repeat to yourself with every exhalation, "peace," "love," "trust," or "patience." Experiment. Try several different words to see what works best for you.

As you begin to practice meditation, you will find that thoughts intrude, and that soon you are off on a thought stream, no longer attending to your breathing and saying the word you chose. That's okay, don't worry about it. When you realize this is happening, just return to paying attention to your breathing and saying the word with each exhalation. As time goes on, and with practice, you will find that intruding thoughts become less of a problem.

After you have practiced this exercise for about ten or fifteen minutes, twice a day, every day for one to two weeks, you will be ready to employ a shortened version of this meditation technique to help you stop the cynical thoughts out there in the real world. When you notice the cynical thoughts starting to build, simply start to meditate *right there,* wherever you are. You don't have to go into a "yoga" position, or close your eyes, or do anything that is going to make you look foolish in public. All you have to do is fix your attention on some object nearby—the elevator button, for example; attend to your breathing; and say your word silently every time you breathe out. Do this until the elevator comes, until you get to the head of the bank or supermarket line—whatever.

This will draw your mind's eye away from the habitual pattern of your cynical thoughts. It will counter the anger you might be feeling, if your thoughts have already progressed to that stage. It will also, as described in Dr. Benson's most recent book, *Your Maximum Mind* (which I can recommend to you as a good source of more detailed information about this meditation technique), calm your cardiovascular system, as well as other bodily systems involved in responding to stress.

You may be wondering at this point about the potential utility of expressing anger, of "getting it out in the open." You may have heard that getting it off your chest can be a cathartic way to deal with anger. You may be worried that what I have been saying might lead dangerously to "bottling up" your anger.

To these concerns I say that I know of no evidence that suggests that letting your anger "show" in frequent outbursts has ever done any long-range good for anyone. The available evidence suggests it is those who say their anger is not bottled up, but out there for all to see, who are at greater risk of harmful health consequences. The problem really isn't so much whether anger shows, but what sponsors it. Anger that is "unrealistic"—that, if expressed, really serves no useful purpose, doesn't correct a situation, since there is nothing "out there" to correct—is the cynical kind of anger that is most troublesome. As we learned from

Dr. Suarez's experiment, this anger is likely only to harm physically the person experiencing it. The resulting aggression, if expressed often enough, moreover serves not to change others' behavior so much as to drive them away, leaving us isolated and alone.

STEP EIGHT: PRACTICE TRUST

I alluded earlier to the potential benefits of trusting other people when I suggested you solicit the help of a spouse or friend in your efforts to develop a more trusting heart. It is a valuable strategy.

Begin by looking for opportunities in which if you trust someone else and it doesn't work out, no real harm is done. For example, if you are a cynical sort, you probably don't trust the airline ticket agent to assign you a good seat—you tell him you want seat 14C. Nor do you trust the person behind the seafood counter at your favorite upscale supermarket to choose the very best tuna steak for you— you point out the very one *you* have decided is the best. (Notice that your lack of trust in others continually forces you to focus on yourself—on the "I," the "me," and the "mine.")

Use such situations to practice trust. When you get up to the check-in counter at the airport, instead of "14C!" try saying, "Oh, whatever seat you pick is fine with me." I'll bet that more times than not, you'll end up in a better seat than the one you would have picked for yourself. (This is the way I discovered that the seats next to the emergency exits have certain advantages, like more leg room and that the seats in front of you don't recline, and in case of an accident you get to be first out.)

And what about that tuna steak? Do you really think you know better than the person who works there, who handles the fish every day, how to pick out a really good piece of tuna? Go ahead, trust him to pick out a good one for you and see what you get. Chances are pretty good it will be better than your choice. And your risk of its being worse is really very small.

And what about that wife who can't cook the spaghetti without it sticking together? Come on, take a chance and try forcing yourself *not* to hover about when she's cooking. *Don't* meticulously inspect every strand when it gets to your plate, ever on guard to reject the stuck-together ones. Instead, read a book while she cooks the spaghetti. Then, when you sit down to eat it, even if half the strands are so stuck together you must use a knife to cut them, force yourself to focus on something else—which, incidentally, can draw attention to more positive aspects of both of your days. What does your wife have to say about her day? What do you have to share about your day?

So what if you have to chew a little harder to get that spaghetti down? What's really more important when you get right down to it: having unstuck spaghetti, or a caring and supportive relationship? (By the way, this exercise works just as well for wives who have "incompetent" husbands; and parents with "incompetent" children.)

Are you beginning to get the idea? Maybe trusting others won't kill you, after all. You'll eat that occasional stuck-together spaghetti, sure, but hardly anyone ever died from that. On the other hand, our research seems to indicate that lots of folks *have died* from their own hostility. And trusting others also tells them—far more convincingly than any words you can utter—that you have confidence in them.

As I said earlier, this gives your children the message that they are capable of doing something right, instead of the message that they can't be trusted to do anything right. If the latter is the message you are sending, they will eventually get the idea, and cease to have confidence in themselves, and to view others as untrustworthy, just as *you* have taught them.

STEP NINE: LEARN TO LISTEN

When you break in on someone during a conversation, it sends the message that *your* ideas are more important than theirs. Done often enough, this habit will cause others to withdraw from you, since by your behavior you are telling them you have no interest in their words or ideas.

To prevent this, learn to listen. If you have to, *force* yourself to keep your mouth shut until they have finished. If what you planned to say is important enough, you'll remember to say it later. (Besides, you might learn something worthwhile while listening.) Last but not least, your attentive posture will send this message to the other person: *I value you and your ideas.* It's irresistible, and will certainly help focus *their* attention on *you* when it's your turn to speak.

STEP TEN: LEARN TO BE ASSERTIVE

When you are truly—that is, realistically, as affirmed by an impartial jury of your peers—being mistreated by another person, what should you do? Any normal human being will become angry when mistreated badly enough. Even Jesus blew his stack when he saw the moneychangers desecrating the Temple.

These are the times when some form of *appropriate response* is not only justified but even necessary. Note I emphasize "appropriate," which does not imply an immediate angry outburst of rage on your part. That hardly ever accomplishes anything constructive, and often escalates the feelings of anger and aggression all around.

If the offending person is not someone with whom you will need to have further contact in the future, the best response is probably simply to put a check beside that person's name in your mental notebook and resolve to have as little to do with him or her in the future as possible. It is hard enough to learn to be more trusting yourself, without having to contend with those others who are unwilling or unable to make the same effort. Still, it will be good practice for you to treat such people as well as you can when it is impossible to avoid them.

But what if the offending person is someone you will not be able to avoid, a close family member, a coworker, or a person who, despite his or her hostility, has other redeeming features that make you want to keep his or her friendship? Here is where the neglected art and science of *assertiveness* comes to the rescue.

It is one thing to lash out aggressively at another in a way that gives him the basic message that he is uniformly bad. It is quite another to inform him, calmly and without rancor, what it is specifically about his *behavior*—notice I said his behavior, not his personality, or his innate selfishness—that is bothering you, and why. This approach has the advantage of providing the other person an attainable goal: even if his personality is pretty well fixed, nearly everyone is capable of changing specific behaviors, especially if you ask in a nice way.

Earlier I gave the example of being assertive in a supermarket line when it is necessary to deal with the objective demands of a situation—it is five-thirty and you have to drive home, dress, and be ready to leave again by six. Another example might serve to illustrate how we can let someone we care about know when something she is doing is upsetting to us.

Let us suppose you are playing tennis with a good friend, a person with whom you have a long-standing, warm, and satisfying relationship.

Let us suppose that despite her generally high level of considerate behavior in other areas, this particular friend has the annoying tennis habit of challenging your calls whenever they go against her: "Are you *sure* that was out? It looked like it got the line to me." Or, "Aw, come on! I saw that hit and I *know* it was in."

Let us suppose also that you are trying to cut down on your own cynicism, anger, and aggressive behavior. Consequently, even though you aren't *saying* anything about her calls, inside you are steaming: Your cynicism "tapes" are running at fast forward and your adrenaline levels are high enough to kill three white rabbits.

And you are just three seconds away from really letting her have it. "You blind bitch," you are about to shout, "where do you get off questioning every call I make that doesn't give you a point, when you can't even make the right call on your side half the time!"

But wait, you've read this book and you know you have another, healthier option. Right you are, and here is how I suggest you handle the situation just outlined, assertively, not aggressively.

First, walk slowly (if you walk too fast, it might betray your pent-up emotions) up to the net and *casually* beckon to your friend to join you. It will help in what follows if you can maintain a relaxed, friendly expression on your face (this may be hard, but give it a try). Then you say to your friend:

> Say, Sally (or Sam), every time, or it seems like every time, I call one of your balls out, you question my call. I'm beginning to feel like you don't trust me to call 'em as honestly as I can. This made me feel hurt at first, but now I'm starting to get riled up.
>
> Now, we don't have any umpire or linesmen out here to call the lines for us, so we have to rely on each

other. I was taught that the drill is for you to call the balls on your side of the net and for me to call the ones on my side. Sure, we may make an occasional mistake, but can't we both assume the other is going to do the best he can, and concentrate on enjoying our game rather than constantly worrying over whether the other guy is going to make a bad call?

If you keep on questioning my calls like you've been doing, I'm going to keep getting angrier and angrier with you. Since I value your friendship too much to want to have that kind of feeling when we are doing something that should be fun, I really do hope you'll be able to trust me to call the lines as honestly and accurately as I can and stop challenging my calls. If this is something you don't feel you can do, that's okay—I'll still love you, but we'll just have to stop trying to play tennis together. Whaddya say?

Let's review the steps you have just taken in being assertive. First, you told her what *behavior* of hers was distressing you. Note well that you did *not* accuse her of being bad or inconsiderate—you simply described your observation of what she had been doing when you called her balls out. Second, you followed that directly with a description of the *feelings* you were experiencing as a result of her behavior. Third, you described what you believe to be the appropriate behavior for the current situation. Fourth, you made a general appeal for her to change her behavior so you could both enjoy the tennis game more. Fifth, you informed her of the consequences of her continuing behavior, both in terms of your worsening feelings (more anger) and your specific behavioral response (no more tennis together). And sixth, you took pains to let her know that you value her and her friendship, and made it clear that this was a rejection of a specific behavior of hers, not of her as a person.

Here's a a more general, all-purpose outline of the important aspects of assertiveness:

*First, take a moment to collect your thoughts, to plan what you will say, and to remind yourself to speak in a pleasant, friendly way.
*Describe, in specific terms, the behavior that distresses you.
*Say as clearly and calmly as you can just what feelings you are experiencing because of the behavior in question.
*Suggest a solution to the problem you have just defined. This will often take the form of a specific request that the other person cease or change the behavior that is causing you to have such unpleasant feelings.
*Inform the other person of the consequences he can expect if he is unwilling to make the change in behavior you are requesting.
*Reassure the other person (assuming this is the case) that you do care for him, value his friendship, and hope your relationship will continue to be satisfying to both of you.
*Ask for his response to what you have proposed, wait patiently for the answer, and listen quietly and carefully, trying as hard as you can to understand what he is saying in response.

You have probably noticed by now that it takes more words to be assertive than it does to let someone know you are angry with him. Okay, I admit it, it *is* more work to be assertive than to be aggressive. In fact, explaining your feelings and what is behind them may not even seem "natural" to you at first. But go ahead, give it a try; there's no time limit. The world won't come to an end, and you may even find that it feels good. Learning to be assertive is very important because it is a constructive alternative to aggression. It just works better, too.

Along with the specific exercises I have suggested to stop your cynical thoughts and the anger and aggression they engender, the day-to-day practice of treating others with trust—kindly and with consideration of their feelings—will, if you stick with it, eventually also help diminish your cynical thoughts, anger, and aggressive outbursts.

This is your long-range goal. When you are just starting out on the path to having a more trusting heart, it might be a good idea, as I said earlier, to avoid folks, even friends, who you know are hostile themselves. Being cynical, quick to anger, and prone to respond aggressively, they will only activate your own similar tendencies and make it harder for you to successfully develop a more trusting heart. Only when your assertiveness skills are honed, when you are able to laugh at your own irrational cynicism, to stop your own hostile thoughts and subsequent anger, to trust that others will behave well and do the best they can—only then might you wish to consider reestablishing contact with such hostile people.

At that time, I recommend that you try to do so, for if you can treat them well, especially if they might genuinely be considered your enemies, you will know you truly have a trusting heart.

STEP ELEVEN: PRETEND TODAY IS YOUR LAST

If you are still finding it hard to effect these suggested changes you might try this strategy: Pretend you have just learned you have a fatal illness. For the moment, let your mind think that you only have a few weeks, days, even one day, to live. Does this make it seem more important to do the things described in this chapter?

If so, and I suspect you will find it easier to be trusting when you adopt this mindset, you might also wish to reflect on this simple truth: We are all afflicted with a "fatal" illness called life. The only difference between most of us and those who have been given the bad news about a fatal illness is that we are less sure about "how much time we have." Now reflect on the idea that all of our past is made up of "moments" like the one we are living right now; and the present moment will be our future's memory. Which would you rather have to look back on in your life—cynical thoughts, angry feelings, and aggressive acts? Or trusting thoughts, joyful feelings, and acts of kindness?

Many times, in interviewing heart patients, when I ask them about anger and how they handle it, I hear, "Oh, I used to get angry a lot, but since my heart attack I've realized that all these nit-picking things that used to rile me so aren't really worth the candle."

Why wait until you've had a heart attack to start doing something about your hostility?

STEP TWELVE: PRACTICE FORGIVING

One final strategy for reducing hostility and having a more trusting heart: Simply *forgive* those who have mistreated and/or angered you. Rather than blame those who have mistreated you, rather than continuing to resent them and to seek revenge, try to understand the emotions of the one who has wronged you. By letting go of the resentment and relinquishing the goal of retribution, you may find, as psychiatrist Richard Fitzgibbons suggests, that the weight of anger lifts from your shoulders, easing your pain and also helping you to forget the wrong.

Use this handy reference guide to help you to remember the twelve strategies to acquiring a trusting heart:

| Step One: | Monitor your cynical thoughts. |
| Step Two: | Confess your hostility and seek support to change. |

Step Three:	Stop cynical thoughts.
Step Four:	Reason with yourself.
Step Five:	Put yourself in the other guy's shoes.
Step Six:	Laugh at yourself.
Step Seven:	Practice the relaxation response.
Step Eight:	Try trusting others.
Step Nine:	Force yourself to listen more.
Step Ten:	Substitute assertiveness for aggression.
Step Eleven:	Pretend today is your last.
Step Twelve:	Practice forgiveness.

A final word: These are steps you can take yourself. Like anyone trying to learn new skills, you may find the going rough at times. You might make better progress with "professional instruction." Most medical schools, and many of our larger hospitals, have rehabilitation programs for heart patients (and wellness programs for healthy folks). If you feel extra help would benefit you, by all means, seek out one of these programs. Many of them employ group sessions, which appear to be effective because they enable hostile persons to realize they are not alone in their cynical beliefs, and to profit from the experiences of others.

TWELVE

THE RELIGIOUS
AND MEDICAL PATHS

THE RELIGIOUS PATH

Since religious teachings share in common the tenet that we should be less concerned with our own needs, our own selves, and more concerned with loving and caring for others, we can certainly rely on these teachings also to guide us toward a trusting heart. Let me point to a few of the obvious ideas the religious teachings offer to those who wish to be more trusting, less angry, and less aggressive.

At the highest level, overarching all details, is the consistent theme that we should treat others with kindness and consideration.

In his letters, Paul offered much practical advice as to how to put this central theme of Jesus' teachings into action in daily life:

Bless those who persecute you; bless and do not curse them. Rejoice with those who rejoice, weep with those who weep. Live in harmony with one another; do not be haughty, but associate with the lowly; never be conceited. Repay no one evil for evil, but take thought for what is noble in the sight of all. If possible, so far as it depends upon you, live peaceably with all. Beloved, never avenge yourselves, but leave it to the wrath of God. . . . No, if your enemy is hungry, feed him; if he is thirsty, give him drink. . . . Do not be overcome by evil, but overcome evil with good. (Romans 12:14–21)

Owe no one anything, except to love one another; for he who loves his neighbor has fulfilled the law. The commandments, "You shall not commit adultery, You shall not kill, You shall not steal, You shall not covet," and any other commandment are summed up in this sentence, "You shall love your neighbor as yourself." Love does no wrong to a neighbor; therefore love is the fulfilling of the law. (Romans 13:8–10)

But now put them all away: anger, wrath, malice, slander, and foul talk from your mouth. Do not lie to one another, seeing that you have put off the old nature with its practices. . . . Put on then, as God's chosen ones, holy and beloved, compassion, kindness, lowliness, meekness, and patience, forbearing one another and, if one has a complaint against another, forgiving each other; as the Lord has forgiven you, so you also must forgive. And above all these put on love, which binds everything together in perfect harmony. (Colossians 3:8–9, 12–14)

Similar advice can be found in the other religious traditions. Let me provide one more example here from Buddhist scriptures:

May I be a protector of the helpless! May I be a guide of wayfarers! May I be like unto a boat, a bridge and a causeway for all who wish to cross! May I be a lamp for all who need a lamp! May I be a bed for all who lack a bed! (*Bodhicaryavatara*, III, 19)

Many religious traditions offer the advice to hold one's tongue. This appears quite sound, when we consider the importance of listening, and that it is so often our words that convey to others our cynical thoughts and angry feelings. Here are some examples from Judaism and Confucianism:

All my days I have grown up among the wise, and I have found nought of better service than silence; not learning but doing is the chief thing; and whoso is profuse of words causes sin. (*Sayings of the Fathers* I, 17)

Silence is good for the wise; how much more so for the foolish . . . Even a fool, when he holdeth his peace, is counted wise. (Proverbs 17:28)

A gentleman covets the reputation of being slow in word but prompt in deed. (*Analects* IV, 24)

A gentleman is ashamed to let his words outrun his deeds. (*Analects* XIV, 29)

The Master said, I would much rather not have to talk. (*Analects* XVII, 19)

In many places there is also found the advice to worry less about the shortcomings of others—all too often the focus of the hostile person's thoughts—and to be more concerned about our own. Here are two examples from the teachings of Jesus and Confucius:

Judge not, that you be not judged. For with the judgment you pronounce you will be judged; and the measure you give will be the measure you get. Why do you see the speck that is in your brother's eye, but do not notice the log that is in your own eye? Or how can you say to your

brother, "Let me take the speck out of your eye," when
there is the log in your own eye? You hypocrite, first take
the log out of your own eye, and then you will see clearly
to take the speck out of your brother's eye. (Matthew
7:1–5)

Attack the evil that is within yourself; do not attack the
evil that is in others. (*Analects* XII, 21)

We can also find advice to avoid the company of those
who are hostile:

The Master said, In the presence of a good man, think all
the time how you may learn to equal him. In the presence
of a bad man, turn your gaze within! (*Analects* IV, 17)

Do not appease thy fellow in the hour of his anger, and
comfort him not in the hour when his dead lies before
him, and question him not in the hour of his vow, and
strive not to see him in the hour of his disgrace. (*Sayings
of the Fathers* IV, 23)

Step twelve of the behavior-modification path is to
forgive those who mistreat us. In *The Perennial Philosophy*,
Aldous Huxley quotes William Law to make a similar point
from the religious perspective:

By considering yourself as an advocate with God for
your neighbors and acquaintances, you would never find
it hard to be at peace with them yourself. . . . Intercession
is the best arbitrator of all differences, the best promoter
of friendship, the best cure and preservative against all
unkind tempers, all angry and haughty passions. . . . You
cannot possibly have any ill-temper or show any unkind
behavior to a man for whose welfare you are so much
concerned, as to be his advocate with God in private. For
you cannot possibly despise and ridicule that man whom
your private prayers recommend to the love and favor of
God.

THE TRUSTING HEART   201

I have only tried here to hint at the possible outlines of the religious paths to a more trusting heart. For those to whom this path appeals as an important means for reducing hostility and becoming a more trusting heart, I advise you to seek out an appropriate spiritual adviser—whether priest, rabbi, or minister—to guide you.

I believe the reasons for pursuing the path offered by one of the world's religions are self-contained within each of their teachings. At the same time, evidence exists that for those who consider religious observance an important part of their lives, there are health benefits.

Studies from Jerusalem's Hadassah University Hospital have found the risk of suffering a heart attack to be over four times higher among Jewish residents of Jerusalem who described themselves as secular than among those who described themselves as religiously orthodox. Studies from this same center also found higher levels of cholesterol among 17- to 18-year-old secular Jerusalem residents than among their religiously orthodox counterparts. These differences could not be explained by differences in dietary fat intake.

Around the world, in Evans County, Georgia, similar results have been obtained. Among those citizens of Evans County who reported frequent attendance at church, blood-pressure levels were lower than among those who attended church less often.

As Dr. Berton Kaplan, my colleague at the University of North Carolina in Chapel Hill, has noted, many aspects of religious observance could be health enhancing and disease preventing. In this book, I have called attention to the fact that many of the world's major religions have as one of their core teachings the injunction to be less concerned with self and more concerned with loving others and treating them well—a set of teachings that parallels what modern research has taught us about the health-promoting effects of a personality profile characterized by more trust, less anger, and less aggression toward our fellow humans.

Thus, it is likely that religious observance does contribute to better health via adherence to the core teachings just enumerated. As Dr. Kaplan notes, however, there are other benefits to be derived from religious observance. These include the social support one can obtain from membership in a caring religious community, and the stress-reducing effects of the prayer and meditation common to all religions, a benefit Dr. Benson has also noted.

Dr. Kaplan also reminds us of the dark places where religion has sometimes led us—the conflicts between Protestant and Catholic in Northern Ireland, between Arab and Jew in the Middle East. How can these effects be reconciled with my major focus?

I can offer no definitive answer to such a question. Nevertheless, I do offer this for your consideration: The evils that have been done in the name of religion are not reflections of their core teachings and philosophies, but, rather, the grafting onto religion of humankind's unfortunate tendencies toward cynical mistrust, anger, and aggression. To the extent that the core teachings and the research on the trusting heart point to the same ideals, perhaps it may help to reduce the wider role cynicism, anger, and aggression have usurped in human discourse and relationships.

THE MEDICAL PATH

You can benefit right now from taking the behavior-modification and religious paths described earlier. In contrast, the major premise that underlies the medical path—that biological correlates of cynicism, anger, and aggression are responsible for their adverse effects on health—is only now being sufficiently worked out in a way that suggests there are applications we can make toward the all-important task of prevention.

The rationale goes like this. If biological characteristics—excessive adrenaline, cortisol, and testosterone responses to stress; inadequate calming-branch "braking action" on the emergency branch's effects—are responsible for the increased risk of disease among hostile persons, then why not use drugs that block those harmful effects and/or mimic the protective effects?

To a certain extent, this is already being done with some success, in the form of beta-blocking drugs that stop the effects of adrenaline on the heart. Almost universally prescribed during the first year following a heart attack, these drugs have been shown to reduce significantly the risk of suffering a second heart attack during that period. It is not clear, however, that their benefit extends beyond the first year; and there is really no available data with which to evaluate the possible benefit of such drugs in preventing a *first* heart attack.

The problems with long-term drug treatment, of course, are the potential unpleasant side effects, as well as actual harmful effects that could cancel out any benefits. For example, although heart disease deaths decreased when drugs were used to lower blood cholesterol levels, death rates due to other causes increased; the net result showed no difference in overall death rates between drug and control groups.

Yet, there is reason to expect that as our knowledge of the biological pathways from hostility to disease becomes more detailed and specific, it will become feasible to design drug approaches that will have a net positive effect on health and longevity, without adverse side effects. While the "side effects" of the Great Fire of 1666 in London were too severe to make it a useful preventive measure, it did stop the plague. With identification of the plague-causing germ, however, it was possible to design public health measures and specific treatments that did not have such disastrous side effects and yet still effectively ended the Black Death.

I can't yet tell you what eventual form the effective and safe drug approaches to prevent the biological consequences of hostility will take, but given the clues provided by the biological research to date, some informed speculation is possible.

It appears likely that excessive cortisol responses (e.g., when hostile people are driven to their frequent experience of anger) increase risk of disease. In recent studies at Duke, we found that pretreatment of young Type A men with *alprazolam*—a new tranquilizer drug useful in treating panic attacks—was effective in completely blocking their cortisol responses to a mental-arithmetic stressor. This does not mean we are ready to put every hostile person on a potent tranquilizer. It does mean that when we are confident enough that excessive cortisol responses are important precursors to disease in hostile persons we should try to develop safe drugs without side effects to block such excesses.

As we refine our ability to identify potential biological precursors of disease in hostile persons, we will certainly consider using very specialized preventive drugs. If, for example, the presence of excessive testosterone and cortisol are found to be important causes of coronary disease in hostile men, *ketoconazole* may prove useful. An oral antifungal agent that cures such infections as athlete's foot and ringworm, ketoconazole has some interesting "side effects": It blocks formation of cortisol in the adrenal gland and of testosterone in the gonads. Eventually, it may be possible to modify the drug and adjust the dosage so that only the "excessive" cortisol and testosterone responses are blocked, leaving normal responses and levels unaffected. In other words, it may be possible for the hostile man to avoid a heart attack without having to pay the price of impotence.

Of course, the first line of attack against the ravages of hostility should be the behavior-modification and religious paths. They are far less likely to do harm than the drug approaches. Yet there is ample precedent for approaches that begin with behavior modification and then progress, if behavior modification doesn't do the job, to drug treatment. This is the case now for both high blood pressure and high blood cholesterol levels: You start with programs for diet, weight loss, salt restriction, exercise, and the like; but if these don't reduce blood pressure or cholesterol to safe levels, you take the next step, drugs. A similar progression may well work to blunt the harm done by a hostile heart.

Finally, there is one more "medical" approach that we can advise without much fear of harm and with the expectation that it will help protect you—exercise. In a series of follow-up studies of college alumni, epidemiologist Dr. Ralph Paffenbarger has found that men who remain more physically active have lowered mortality rates when compared to their more sedentary counterparts.

Dr. James Blumenthal has been carrying out several studies at Duke to evaluate the effects of aerobic fitness training upon cardiovascular responses to stress. In comparison to folks who engage only in strength training, he finds that those who engage in jogging at levels sufficient to increase aerobic fitness become less responsive, in terms of heart rate and blood pressure, to mental arithmetic stress.

It may be hard for some of you to change. Despite your now detailed knowledge of the health consequences and the firmest resolve to be less hostile, you may still find the cynical thoughts cropping up, the anger rising, and the aggression erupting. If this is the case for you, I encourage you to persist, and persist some more. There are many suggestions in this book; at least some of them, over time, *will* work for you. Trust me!

EPILOGUE

SOME FINAL THOUGHTS: IS WHAT IS GOOD FOR INDIVIDUALS GOOD FOR GROUPS?

I n the 1960s, many Americans began to rely less on societal and cultural norms and more on personal needs, wants, and desires as the most valid guide for their behavior. This trend culminated in the 1980s, when even greed became an acceptable guiding principle—reflected in the standing ovation a university audience accorded Ivan Boesky when he proclaimed that greed is great. Somehow, we had come to expect we should be able to have and do whatever we wanted, whenever we wanted.

A corollary of this trend has been the tendency of groups—whether defined along national lines or in terms of groups within a single nation—to view other groups with cynical mistrust, and often to act on the basis of this attitude; perhaps the expression of the fear that what one group or nation gets means less for *my* group or *my* nation.

Now, as the 1980s draw to a close, there seems to be

a collective turning away from such self-centeredness and cynicism. This new direction appears to be spurred by many recent events taken together: a general revulsion at the Wall Street insider-trading scandals, the excesses of the televangelists, and the activities of some government officials involved in various scandals, as well as, perhaps, our growing collective dissatisfaction with those in our society who seem to find enemies on every side. It's no way to live.

Would the development of a more trusting heart in each of us accelerate—on a community, national, or even international scale—this movement away from self-centeredness and cynicism?

Is it possible that self-centeredness, cynicism, anger, and aggression are as harmful for the body politic as they are for the body physical?

These are questions I cannot answer at the scientific level. I nonetheless commend them as worthy of your attention.

What I can do, in closing, is wish you success in your own efforts to develop a trusting heart.

SOURCES AND NOTES

This book is based on epidemiological and laboratory research findings. Most of the research described has already been published in scientific journals, and that which has not yet been published has been presented at a national scientific meeting. Thus, whenever I describe a specific research result in the text, it is based on scientific work that has been through a review process before it has been published or presented at a scientific meeting.

Rather than distract the reader with frequent footnotes to these sources in the text, I have chosen instead to provide the citations in this section, with each citation given according to the chapter and page number where the material based on it appears. This will enable those readers wishing more details to go to the original scientific reports.

Another purpose served by this section is to provide interested readers with more details regarding some points

made in the text. These details are not essential for understanding those points, but they do provide a bit of amplifi-
cation and further illustrations that could help some
readers grasp the points more completely.

Introduction

page xi   "spend billions": Barsky, A. J. "The Paradox of
Health." *The New England Journal of Medicine*, 1988, vol. 318,
pp. 414–18.

page xii "reports began to appear": See Fischman, Joshua, "Type
A on Trial," in *Psychology Today*, February 1987, pp. 42–50,
for a good example.

1. ". . . But Words Can Also Hurt Me"

page 3 "It had been a quiet morning": This material is based on
"Case Records of the Massachusetts General Hospital" (Case
18-1986), *The New England Journal of Medicine*, 1986, vol. 314,
pp. 1240–47.

page 10 "Type As actually lived *longer*": Ragland, D. R., and
Brand, R. J. "Type A Behavior and Mortality from Coronary Heart Disease." *The New England Journal of Medicine*,
1988, vol. 318, pp. 65–69.

2. From Anecdote to Epidemiology

page 15 "Framingham Study": More details are in Dawber, T. R.,
*The Framingham Study: The Epidemiology of Atherosclerotic Dis-
ease*. Cambridge: Harvard University Press, 1980.

page 18 "Sir John Hunter": Williams, J., and Edwards, G. "The
Death of John Hunter." *Journal of the American Medical Association*, 1968, vol. 204, pp. 806–809.

page 19 "von Deusch": von Deusch, T. *Lehrbuch der Herzkrank-
heiten*. Leipzig: Verlag von Wilhelm Engelman, 1868.

page 19 "Sir William Osler": Two good sources for Osler's observations on the role of mental factors in coronary disease are
"The Lumleian Lectures on Angina Pectoris." *The Lancet*,
March 12 and 26, April 9, 1910; and *Lectures on Angina Pectoris
and Allied States*. New York: Appleton, 1892.

page 21 "Friedman and Rosenman became convinced": A good

description of their early work on Type A can be found in Friedman, M., and Rosenman, R. *Type A Behavior and Your Heart*. New York: Knopf, 1974.

page 24 "conduct the Western Collaborative Group Study": Rosenman, R.; Brand, R. J.; Jenkins, C. D.; Friedman, M.; Straus, R.; and Wurm, M. "Coronary Heart Disease in the Western Collaborative Group Study: Final Follow-up Experience of 8½ Years." *Journal of the American Medical Association*, 1975, vol. 233, pp. 872–77.

pages 29–31 The three studies from Duke, Columbia, and Boston University were: Blumenthal, J. A.; Williams, R. B.; Kong, Y.; Schanberg, S. M.; and Thompson, L. W. "Type A Behavior Pattern and Coronary Atherosclerosis." *Circulation*, 1978, vol. 58, pp. 634–39; Frank, K. A.; Heller, S. S.; Kornfeld, D. S.; Sporne, A. A.; and Weiss, M. B. "Type A Behavior Pattern and Coronary Angiographic Findings." *Journal of the American Medical Association*, 1978, vol. 240, pp. 761–63; and Zyzanski, S. J.; Jenkins, C. D.; Ryan, T. J.; Flessas, A.; and Everist, M. "Psychological Correlates of Coronary Angiographic Findings." *Archives of Internal Medicine*, vol. 136, pp. 1234–37.

page 32 "meeting in St. Petersburg": Dembroski, T. M.; Weiss, S. M.; Shields, J. L.; Haynes, S. G.; and Feinleib, M., eds. *Coronary-Prone Behavior*. New York: Springer-Verlag, 1978.

3. Euphoria Gives Way to Uncertainty

page 34 "blue-ribbon panel": The Review Panel on Coronary-Prone Behavior and Coronary Heart Disease. "Coronary-Prone Behavior and Coronary Heart Disease: A Critical Review." *Circulation*, 1981, vol. 63, pp. 1199–1215.

page 34 "minor annoyances": Dimsdale, J. E.; Hackett, T. P.; Hutter, A. M.; Block, P. C.; Catanzano, D. M.; and White, P. J. "Type A Personality and Extent of Coronary Atherosclerosis." *American Journal of Cardiology*, 1978, vol. 43, pp. 583–88.

page 34 "Jenkins Activity Survey": Jenkins, C. D. "A Comparative Review of the Interview and Questionnaire Methods in the Assessment of the Coronary-Prone Behavior Pattern." In Dembroski, T. M.; Weiss, S. M.; Shields, J. L.; Haynes,

S. G.; and Feinleib, M., eds. *Coronary-Prone Behavior.* New York: Springer-Verlag, 1978

page 35 "Aspirin Myocardial Infarction Study": Shekelle, R. B.; Gale, M.; and Norusis, M. "Type A Behavior (Jenkins Activity Survey) and Risk of Recurrent Coronary Heart Disease in the Aspirin Myocardial Infarction Study." *American Journal of Cardiology,* 1985, vol. 56, pp. 221–25.

page 35 "other large research studies": Case, R. B.; Heller, S. S.; Case, N. B.; and Moss, A. J. "Type A Behavior and Survival After Acute Myocardial Infarction." *The New England Journal of Medicine,* 1985, vol. 312, pp. 634–39. The drug chosen for use in this study was propranolol (Inderal), which blocks the effects of adrenaline on beta-receptors. This could be helpful in reducing the harmful effects of adrenaline to increase the work load on the heart and to make the heart more likely to develop life-threatening rhythm disturbances.

pages 36–37 "MRFIT": Shekelle, R. B.; Hulley, S.; Neaton, J.; Billings, J.; Borhani, N.; Gerace, T.; Jacobs, D.; Lasser, N.; Mittlemark, M.; Stamler, J.; and the MRFIT Research Group. "The MRFIT Behavioral Pattern Study: II. Type A Behavior Pattern and Incidence of Coronary Heart Disease." *American Journal of Epidemiology,* 1985, vol. 122, pp. 559–70.

page 37 "several additional . . . studies": For a detailed review of the negative studies on Type A, see Matthews, K. A., and Haynes, S. G. "Type A Behavior Pattern and Coronary Risk: Update and Critical Evaluation." *American Journal of Epidemiology,* 1986, vol. 123, pp. 23–96.

page 38 "Dr. Marcia Angell concluded": Angell, M. "Disease as a Reflection of the Psyche." *The New England Journal of Medicine,* 1985, vol. 312, pp. 1570–72.

page 38 "attacks in professional journals": I and three other past-presidents of the Society of Behavioral Medicine responded to the Angell editorial in a letter to the editor that was published in the November 21, 1987, issue of *The New England Journal of Medicine.*

page 39 "my own research at Duke": Williams, R. B.; Barefoot, J. C.; Haney, T. L.; Harrell, F. E.; Blumenthal, J. A.; Pryor, D. B.; and Peterson, B. "Type A Behavior and Angiographically Documented Coronary Atherosclerosis in a Sample of 2,289 patients." *Psychosomatic Medicine*, 1988, vol. 50, pp. 139–52.

page 39 "survival effects": This weakening or reversal of the relation between risk factors and likelihood of disease has been reported already among the Framingham residents for both cholesterol and smoking. Above age 65, it is impossible to show that these "risk factors" predict increased risk, and, above age 70, there is even a reduced mortality rate among those who are smokers. This does not necessarily mean that smoking is no longer harmful after age 70, but, rather, that those smokers who survive to that venerable age are likely to be tough cookies whose strong constitutions enabled them to resist developing a fatal disease earlier in life.

page 39 "leaving only the resistant ones": Another example of these survival effects can be seen in the annual death rates for men aged 45–54 during the first thirty years of the twentieth century. As reported in the U.S. *Vital Statistics*, there was a sharp increase in death rates for these men in 1918. This increase was due, of course, to the disastrous influenza epidemic that killed millions of people worldwide in that year. For the three years following 1918, however, there was a large *decrease* in annual death rates for this same cohort of men. Survival effects were at work: The biologically weak men nearly all succumbed to the influenza in 1918, leaving the hardy men to be a far larger proportion of the population than they had been prior to 1918. With the male population aged 45–54 containing such a larger proportion of hardy individuals post-1918, it is not hard to understand why the death rates dropped.

page 41 "Dimsdale put it well": Dimsdale, J. E. "A Perspective on Type A Behavior and Coronary Disease." (Editorial) *The New England Journal of Medicine*, 1988, vol. 318, pp. 110–12.

4. About Hostility and Type A

page 49 "Cook and Medley": Cook, W., and Medley, D. "Proposed Hostility and Pharasaic-virtue Scales for the MMPI." *Journal of Applied Psychology*, 1954, vol. 38, pp. 414–18. As described in this paper, Drs. Cook and Medley intended their scale to be a measure of "hostility," but, as we shall see, what it actually measures appears to be more complex than the meaning conveyed by this single word.

Cook and Medley used a combination of techniques to develop their scale. First, they used what is called a "rational content analysis" to identify good candidate items for inclusion on the scale: Several psychologists read all 560 MMPI items and marked those they felt to reflect "hostility." This provided a large number of items from which Cook and Medley could choose the ones for final inclusion.

To guide their choice, they had a group of teachers answer True or False to all the candidate items and also to fill out another psychological test, the Minnesota Teacher Attitude Inventory, or MTAI. The MTAI had been developed earlier to measure the degree to which teachers got along well with their students. A high score indicated good teacher-student rapport, while a low score identified those teachers who got along less well with their students.

To decide the final fifty items to include on their Ho scale, Drs. Cook and Medley selected those items that were most often answered the same way by teachers who score lowest on the MTAI. In other words, the final fifty items on the Ho scale were chosen to provide the best possible measure of how well a teacher would get along with his or her pupils, as indicated by the MTAI. The rationale here was that those teachers with poorer rapport would be the most "hostile."

It is not surprising, when we consider its origins, therefore, that the Ho scale measures not a simple, single facet of personality, but a combination of related characteristics.

page 50 "When we compared": This study was reported in Williams, R. B.; Haney, T. L.; Lee, K. L.; Kong, Y.; Blumenthal, J.; and Whalen, R. "Type A Behavior, Hostility, and Coronary Athersclerosis." *Psychosomatic Medicine*, 1980, vol. 42, pp. 539–49.

In this study we also found that higher Ho scores were associated with more severe arteriosclerosis not only in men, but in women patients as well. The same holds true for Type A in our most recent report of findings in 2,289 patients.

Most of the research into the relationship between psychological factors and coronary disease has focused on men, because men are far more likely to develop heart disease, especially during their thirties and forties. Given the significant relationship of Type A and hostility measures to heart disease severity in the studies we have done, I am confident that the relationships I describe for men probably hold equally true for women, but with a ten- to fifteen-year time lag—the result of the hormonal protection enjoyed by women until menopause, after which their coronary disease rates rise to equal those of men.

Another source of protection for women may come from their lower hostility levels and lower levels of Type A behavior, both of which may also be due to hormonal factors: Women lack the high testosterone levels that may make some men more hostile and more Type A.

It will be important in future research to understand more about the role of hostility as a contributor to increased disease risk in women. For the time being, however, there will probably be a bigger and quicker payoff from studies in men, since they are more likely to suffer the premature health problems that appear to result from too much hostility.

page 53 "Western Electric Study": Shekelle, R. B.; Gale, M.; Ostfeld, A. M.; and Paul, O. "Hostility, Risk of Coronary Disease, and Mortality." *Psychosomatic Medicine*, 1983, vol. 45, pp. 219–28.

page 55 "255 doctors": Barefoot, J. C.; Dahlstrom, W. G.; and Williams, R. B. "Hostility, CHD Incidence, and Total Mortality: A 25-year Follow-up Study of 255 Physicians." *Psychosomatic Medicine*, 1983, vol. 45, pp. 59–63.

page 56 "impact of Ho scores upon mortality was even more striking": The much stronger impact of Ho scores on coronary disease and death rates among the UNC doctors than the Western Electric employees appears to be another example of the ubiquitous survival effect. Recall that smoking and high cholesterol levels are far weaker predictors of heart problems among older than among younger persons, and that this weakening of the predictive power of these risk

factors among older groups has been ascribed to the action
of survival effects: In the older groups one is dealing with a
group of hardy survivors, those vulnerable to a given risk
factor having died earlier.

The men in the Western Electric Study were 45–50
years old when that study began in the late 1950s, compared
to the UNC doctors who were only 25 when they completed
the MMPIs in medical school at about the same time. Thus,
the Western Electric Study *began* with men who were about
the same ages as the UNC doctors were at the end of the
twenty-five-year follow-up period depicted in Figure 4-3.
When we see how many of the doctors with high Ho scores
were dead by age 50, it is hard to escape the impression that
those who died probably had predisposing biological factors
that made them, among all those with high Ho scores, most
susceptible to illness. By the same logic, those with high Ho
scores who survived are probably those who were hardier—
who had fewer of the predisposing biological factors that
brought down many of the doctors with higher Ho scores.

Thus, a study beginning, like the Western Electric
Study, with men aged 45–50 would no longer have available
those high Ho scorers with higher biological vulnerability—
those who made up the 14 percent who died prior to age 50
in Figure 4-3.

This relative hardiness of the survivors could account
for the smaller adverse effect of high Ho scores on the Western Electric Study participants from age 50 to 70 than in the
UNC doctors from age 25 to 50. The same principle accounts
for the dip in death rates from 1919 to 1923: The weakest
segment of the population died off during the 1918 influenza
epidemic, leaving a group of survivors that was unusually
hardy.

page 56 "two additional studies": McCranie, E. W.; Watkins, L.;
Brandsma, J.; and Sisson, B. "Hostility, Coronary Heart Disease Incidence, and Total Mortality: Lack of Association in
a 25-year Follow-up Study of 478 Physicians." *Journal of
Behavioral Medicine*, 1986, vol. 9, pp. 119–25, reports a failure
of Ho scores to predict illness and death in physicians who
graduated from the Medical College of Georgia. (MCG).

This study was similar in many respects to the study John Barefoot, Grant Dahlstrom, and I did with UNC medical graduates.

To everyone's surprise, neither coronary events nor deaths due to all causes were predicted by the Ho scores of these MCG graduates. At first this was very distressing, since it appeared that the Ho scale, and our hostility hypothesis, might be going the way of Type A.

One of the advantages of using a psychometric approach, however, is that these questionnaires do not rely upon someone's subjective judgments of behavior during an interview. Rather, they produce numbers that can be examined, not only to determine whether disease is predicted, but to see what went wrong when the expected predictions fail to materialize.

On the very first reading of the MCG paper it was clear that there was at least one critical difference from the UNC study in terms of how the MMPIs were administered. At UNC the medical students were on their psychiatry rotation when, as a class exercise to familiarize them with psychological testing procedures, they were given the MMPI to fill out. They were told that the results would have no effect on their grades, and that the results might be kept for some later, unspecified research purpose.

The MCG doctors were asked to fill out their MMPIs under very different circumstances. First of all, the MMPIs were not given to students who were already admitted to MCG, but to *applicants* for admission, during their visit for interviews that would determine whether they were to be admitted. There is no record of what the applicants were told when they were handed the MMPI forms to fill out.

It is not hard to guess what must have gone through their minds. "Here I am trying to put my best foot forward to get into medical school, and now they are giving me this psychological test. I'd better be careful how I answer these questions!"

But with a psychometric approach using a standardized test like the MMPI, even twenty-five years later, we don't have to guess at their test-taking attitude. The MMPI has "validity" scales that enable trained psychologists to determine whether those being tested have answered the questions truthfully, or whether the answers given are tilted in a way that indicates the first priority of the test taker is to make a good impression.

The results clearly showed that the MCG applicants were trying to put their best foot forward. Their validity scale scores were very high, in the direction termed "faking good." Not very surprisingly, they also have very low scores on the Ho scale, far lower in fact than the UNC medical students. It is easy to understand why someone trying hard to get into medical school would want to deny any negative or antisocial characteristics.

This problem does not mean that the MMPI Ho scale cannot be used as a predictor of disease risks. Like any assessment tool in medicine, the conditions under which it is used must be carefully specified. Blood tests for lipids or glucose levels are important tests in medicine, to assess heart disease risk and to make the diagnosis of diabetes. Yet these "objective" blood tests cannot be accepted as valid under certain conditions, for example, after eating a large meal. This does not mean the blood tests are never valid, just that they are not valid under certain conditions.

Similarly, we cannot rely upon the validity of a psychological test given to a group of young men who have good reason to believe that their answers might influence a major life choice. Thus, it appears upon closer inspection that the MCG failure to confirm the UNC results is not a serious challenge to the hostility hypothesis, since the test-taking situation affected the HO scores that were obtained.

This criticism does not appear to apply, however, to a second study that also failed to find Ho scores predicting heart problems or total death rates. Presented by Dr. Gloria Leon and her colleagues from the University of Minnesota at the 1987 annual meeting of the American Psychosomatic Society in Philadelphia, this study examined the prediction of health problems by Ho scores obtained from MMPIs administered to Minnesota businessmen over thirty years ago.

In contrast to the MCG doctors, there was no reason to

expect that the Minnesota businessmen were under any pressure to make a good impression. This was reflected in more or less "normal" scores on the validity scales that had detected the MCG applicants' efforts to "fake good." Despite these normal validity-scale scores, the middle-aged businessmen scored very low on the Ho scale, lower, in fact, than the MCG applicants. Thus, it appeared that these men were answering the questions as truthfully as they could, but that, as a group, they just naturally had very low Ho scores.

Whereas the MCG study failed to find Ho predicting health problems because the test-taking conditions led to invalid Ho scores, it seems likely that the Minnesota businessmen's study failed to find a Ho effect because *there were too few hostile men for an effect to show up.*

In any epidemiological sample used to identify risk factors for any disease, it is essential for the characteristic being evaluated for risk factor status to be present in enough of the people in the sample for its toxic effects to be seen. For example, if blood cholesterols are determined in a group of several hundred men, and only a few have levels over 200, there is no way that the coronary risk associated with cholesterol levels over 250 can be found in this group.

It seems reasonable to conclude, therefore, that Ho scores failed to predict disease in the Minnesota businessmen because there were too few men in the group with high Ho scores for the toxic effects associated with high Ho scores to show up. Another reason may be the older age of this sample (you will recall that all risk factors are weaker predictors among older groups).

page 58 "Dr. Karen Matthews": Matthews, K. A.; Glass, D. C.; Rosenman, R. H.; and Bortner, R. W. "Competetive Drive, Pattern A, and Coronary Heart Disease: A Further Analysis of Some Data from the Western Collaborative Group Study." *Journal of Chronic Diseases,* 1977, vol. 30, pp. 489–98.

page 59 "component scoring technique": A more complete description can be found in Dembroski, T. M., and Costa, P. T. "Coronary Prone Behavior: Components of the Type A Pattern and Hostility." *Journal of Personality,* 1987, vol. 52, pp. 211–36.

Some cautionary notes are in order, however, for those who might try to use this scoring technique solely on the basis of having read about it. While easy to describe in words, the competent use of this scoring technique requires extensive training, so that the often subtle cues used to detect hostility are not missed. Once this training has been absorbed, researchers are able to use the components-scoring approach to provide reliable measures of hostility, as indicated by close agreement between two trained raters scoring the same interview and by good agreement between the hostility scores of the same person in interviews administered on two separate occasions.

page 59 "a collaborative study": The findings were published in Dembroski, T. M.; MacDougall, J. M.; Williams, R. B.; Haney, T. L.; and Blumenthal, J. A. "Components of Type A, Hostility, and Anger in Relationship to Angiographic Findings." *Psychosomatic Medicine,* 1985, vol. 47, pp. 210–33.

Although Potential for Hostility was significantly correlated with severity of arterial blockages in this study, the overall Type A assessment was not. This was not surprising, since we only included 131 patients in the analysis, a number far too small to permit detection of the small Type A effect that we found in our study of a much larger sample (see p. 39). Since Potential for Hostility did relate significantly to disease severity, even with this small sample of patients, it increased our confidence that hostility is more strongly related to disease than the overall set of characteristics that combine to make up the Type A behavior pattern.

page 60 "performed similar ratings": MacDougall, J. M.; Dembroski, T. M.; Dimsdale, J. E.; and Hackett, T. "Components of Type A, Hostility, and Anger-in: Further Relationships to Angiographic Findings." *Health Psychology,* 1985, vol. 4, pp. 137–52.

page 62 "Drs. Margaret Chesney and Michael Hecker": Hecker, M.; Chesney, M.; Black, G.; and Frautschi, N. "Coronary-prone Behaviors in the Western Collaborative Group Study." *Psychosomatic Medicine,* 1988, vol. 50, pp. 153–64.

page 63 "Dembroski performed a similar analysis": Dembroski,

T. M.; MacDougall, J. M.; Costa, P. T.; and Grandits, G. A. "Antagonistic Hostility as a Predictor of Coronary Heart Disease in the Multiple Risk Factor Intervention Trial." This paper has been submitted for publication and is under review at the time of this writing.

page 64 "self-references": Scherwitz, L.; McKelvain, R.; Laman, C.; Patterson, J.; Dutton, L.; Yusim, S.; Lester, J.; Kraft, I.; Rochelle, D.; and Leachman, R. "Type A Behavior, Self-involvement, and Coronary Atherosclerosis." *Psychosomatic Medicine*, 1983, vol. 45, pp. 47–56.

page 66 "Dr. Timothy Smith": Smith, T. W., and Frohm, K. D. "What's So Unhealthy about Hostility? Construct Validity and Psychosocial Correlates of the Cook and Medley Ho Scale." *Health Psychology*, 1985, vol. 4, pp. 503–20.

page 66 "Alameda County": for a comprehensive description of all the Alameda County Study results, see Berkman, L. F. and Breslow, L., *Health and Ways of Living: The Alameda County Study*, 1983. New York: Oxford University Press.

page 67 "118 lawyers": Barefoot, J. C.; Dodge, K. A.; Peterson, B. L.; Dahlstrom, W. G.; and Williams, R. B. "Predicting Mortality from Scores on the Cook-Medley Scale: A Follow-up Study of 118 Lawyers." Paper presented at the annual meeting of the American Psychosomatic Society, Philadelphia, March 1988. (It will soon be published in *Psychosomatic Medicine*.)

5. From Mind to Body

page 72 "research team at the Bowman-Gray School": A good overview of this important research, along with further references to the specific research papers, can be found in Manuck, S. B.; Kaplan, J. R.; and Matthews, K. A. "Behavioral Antecedents of Coronary Heart Disease and Atherosclerosis." *Atherosclerosis*, 1986, vol. 6, pp. 2–14.

page 82 "differences in physiological responses alone between Type A and Type B men": Rather than cite separately each study of physiologic reactivity, for those readers interested in learning about this area in greater depth the following reviews will serve as a guide to this large research area. Houston, B. K. "Psychophysiological Reactivity and the

Type A Behavior Pattern." *Journal of Research in Personality*, 1983, vol. 17, pp. 22–39. Krantz, D. S., and Manuck, S. B. "Acute Psychophysiologic Reactivity and the Risk of Cardiovascular Disease: A Review and Methodologic Critique." *Psychological Bulletin*, 1984, vol. 96, pp. 435–64. Williams, R. B. "Biological Mechanisms Mediating the Relationship Between Behavior and Coronary Heart Disease." In Siegman, A. W., and Dembroski, T. M., eds. *In Search of Coronary Prone Behavior.* Hillsdale, N.J.: Lawrence Earlbaum, 1988. In addition to the above review papers, there is an entire book that reviews this area: Matthews, K. A.; Weiss, S. M.; Detre, T.; Dembroski, T. M.; Falkner, B.; Manuck, S. B.; and Williams, R. B. *Handbook of Stress, Reactivity, and Cardiovascular Disease.* New York: Wiley, 1986.

page 82 "subjecting Type A and B men": For the most part, this research has focused on physiological responses to stress in men, since it is men who account for most of the premature coronary disease, as well as that predicted by Type A and hostility. Nevertheless, as I pointed out in footnotes to chapter 4, women do appear susceptible to the adverse effects of Type A behavior and hostility, albeit at a later age than their male counterparts. It is not surprising, therefore, that most of the research on biological mechanisms of Type A behavior and hostility has been carried out in men. There are, however a few studies of women. By and large, these have failed to find differences between Type A and B, high- and low-hostility groups. It is likely that this research has not been as carefully pursued as that using male subjects, and that when, as in Ed Suarez's study (described later in chapter 5), appropriate stressors are used, this research will find potentially pathogenic physiological responses in Type A and hostile women.

page 87 "In my first study": Williams, R. B.; Lane, J. D.; Kuhn, C. M.; Melosh, W.; White, A. D.; and Schanberg, S. M. "Type A Behavior and Elevated Physiological and Neuroendocrine Responses to Cognitive Tasks." *Science*, 1982, vol. 218, pp. 483–85.

page 90 "We still do not have a complete understanding": For a review of the currently accepted theory, see Ross, R., and

Glomset, J. A. "The Pathogenesis of Atherosclerosis (Parts I and II)." *The New England Journal of Medicine*, 1976, vol. 295, pp. 369–77, 420–25.

page 91 "excess cortisol has been found": Sprague, E. A.; Troxler, R. G.; Peterson, D. F.; Schmidt, R. E.; and Young, J. T. "Effect of Cortisol on the Development of Arthrosclerosis in Cynomolgus Monkeys." In Kalter, S. S., ed. *The Use of Nonhuman Primates in Cardiovascular Diseases.* Austin, University of Texas Press, 1980.

page 91 "administration of extra testosterone": Uzunova, A. D.; Ramey, E. R.; and Ramwell, P. W. "Gonadal Hormones and Pathogenesis of Occlusive Arterial Thrombosis." *American Journal of Physiology*, 1978, vol. 234, pp. 454–59.

page 94 "bypassed the black box": Muranaka, M.; Monou, H.; Lane, J. D.; Anderson, N. B.; Kuhn, C. M.; Schanberg, S. M.; McCown, N.; Suzuki, J.; and Williams, R. B. "Physiological Responses to Catecholamine Infusions in Type A and B Men." *Health Psychology*, 1988, in press.

page 100 "The basic biology of how this is accomplished": When beta receptors are stimulated, e.g., by isoproterenol infusions, cyclic AMP is formed inside the cell, and its subsequent actions are responsible for what we see as beta adrenergic effects on body functions: heart muscle cells beating harder and faster. The analogous "second messenger" for the acetylcholine muscarinic receptor is cyclic GMP. When the calming branch releases acetylcholine, it stimulates muscarinic receptors, causing cyclic GMP to be formed inside the cells. If those cells are also stimulated by the sympathetic branch, the cyclic GMP formed by the calming branch's action has a very interesting effect: It stimulates an enzyme inside the cell that effectively "chews up" the sympathetic branch's second messenger, cyclic AMP. Thus, when both beta and muscarinic receptors are stimulated on the same cell, let us say a heart muscle cell, the effects of the beta receptor to make that cell contract harder or faster are stopped when the cyclic GMP formed by the calming branch's muscarinic receptor stops the actions of the cyclic AMP that was formed by the sympathetic branch's beta receptor.

page 101 "another study": Muranaka, M.; Lane, J. D.; Suarez, E. C.; Anderson, N. B.; Suzuki, J.; and Williams, R. B. "Stimulus-Specific Patterns of Cardiovascular Reactivity in Type A and B Subjects: Evidence for Enhanced Vagal Reactivity in Type B." *Psychophysiology*, 1988, vol. 25, pp. 330–38.

page 105 "the brainchild of Dr. Edward Suarez": Suarez, E. S.; McRae, A.; and Williams, R. B. "High Scores on the Cook and Medley Hostility (Ho) Scale Predict Increased Cardiovascular Responses to Harassment." Paper presented at the annual meeting of the American Psychosomatic Society, Toronto, March 1988.

6. The Origins of Hostility

page 110 "Erik Erikson": *Childhood and Society.* New York: Norton, 1963.

page 111 "babies are capable of learning": Reported by Gina Kolata in *Science*, 1987, vol. 237, p. 726.

page 112 "rat pups separated": For a review of this important body of research, wherein results from animal studies are applied directly to a major health problem in humans, see Schanberg, S. M., and Field, T. M. "Sensory Deprivation Stress and Supplemented Stimulation in the Rat Pup and Preterm Human Neonate." *Child Development*, 1987, vol. 58, pp. 1431–47.

page 113 "Yet another study": Meaney, M. J.; Aitken, D. H.; van Berkel, C.; Bhatnagar, S.; and Sapolsky, R. M. "Effect of Neonatal Handling on Age-Related Impairments Associated with the Hippocampus." *Science*, 1988, vol. 239, pp. 766–68.

page 113 *"The case of Japan"*: The research results described in this section are all to be found in Stevenson, H.; Azuma, H.; and Hakuta, K., eds. *Child Development and Education in Japan.* New York: W. H. Freeman & Company, 1986.

page 114 "preliminary look": Doba, N.; Hinohara, S.; and Williams, R. B. "Studies on Type A Behavior Pattern and Hostility in Japanese Male Subjects with Special Reference to CHD." *Japanese Journal of Psychosomatic Medicine*, 1983, vol. 23, pp. 321–28.

pages 117–18 "our expectations of others": These studies are described in Jones, E. E. "Interpreting Interpersonal Behavior: The Effects of Expectancies." *Science*, 1986, vol. 234, pp. 41–46.

page 118 "the face we present": Ekman, P.; Friesen, W. V.; and O'Sullivan. "Universals and Cultural Differences in the Judgements of Facial Expressions of Emotion." *Journal of Personality and Social Psychology*, 1987, vol. 53, pp. 712–17.

page 120 *"disgust* in the Type A men": Personal communication from Margaret Chesney, May 1988; a paper describing this research is currently under review.

page 120 "Matthews and her coworkers": For a review of this research area, see Matthews, K. A., and Woodall, K. L. "Childhood Origins of Overt Type A Behaviors and Cardiovascular Reactivity to Behavioral Stressors." *Annals of Behavioral Medicine*, 1988, vol. 10, pp. 71–77.

page 121 "Minnesota study of identical twins": For a review of the heritability of personality factors, see Holden, C. "The Genetics of Personality." *Science*, 1987, vol. 237, pp. 598–601.

page 123 "At NIMH Burr extended": Eichelman, B. "Neurochemical Bases of Aggressive Behavior." *Psychiatric Annals*, 1987, vol. 17, pp. 371–74.

page 124 "Panksepp has proposed": Panksepp, J. "The Psychobiology of Prosocial Behaviors: Separation Distress, Play, and Altruism." In Zahn-Waxler, C.; Cummings, E. M.; and Iannotti, R., eds. *Altruism and Aggression: Biological and Social Origins.* Cambridge: Cambridge University Press, 1986. (This book is an excellent general source for those desiring more information on the origins of hostility, anger, and aggression.)

page 126 "opioids can protect the heart": Verrier, R. L., and Lown, B. "Autonomic Nervous System and Malignant Cardiac Arrhythmias." In Weiner, H.; Hofer, M. A.; and Stunkard, A. J., eds. *Brain, Behavior, and Bodily Disease.* New York: Raven Press, 1981.

page 127 "Kagan has been studying": For a review of Dr. Kagan's research on shyness, see Kagan, J.; Reznick, J. S.; and Snidman, N. "Biological Bases of Childhood Shyness." *Science*, 1988, vol. 240, pp. 167–71.

7. Parallels in World Religions

page 135 "Hillel . . . replied": Hertz, J. H., commentary. *Sayings of the Fathers (Pirke Aboth)*. New York: Behrman House, 1945.

page 137 *"Buddhism"*: The Buddhist scriptures quoted in this section are taken from the following sources: Conze, E., ed. *Buddhist Texts Through the Ages*. Oxford: Casirer, 1954; Woodward, F. L., translator. *Some Sayings of the Buddha*. Oxford: Oxford University Press, 1951; Sangharakshita, B. *A Survey of Buddhism*. Bangalore, India: The Indian Institute of World Culture, W. Q. Judge Press, 1957.

page 141 "the basic scripture of Confucianism": Waley, A., translator. *The Analects of Confucius*. New York: Modern Library Paperbacks (Random House), 1938.

page 144 *"Taoism"*: My source for the Taoist texts I quoted here was "Taoism," in *The New Encyclopaedia Britannica*. Chicago: Encyclopaedia Britannica, Inc., 1986, pp. 394–407.

page 146 "It is a little embarrassing": Huxley, L. A. *This Timeless Moment: A Personal View of Aldonous Huxley*. New York: Farrar, Straus & Giroux, 1968, p. 117.

page 147 "When a finger points": Sangharakshita, B., op. cit., p. 213.

8. Before We Start

page 152 "the Recurrent Coronary Prevention Project": Friedman, M.; Thoresen, C. E.; Gill, J. J.; et al., "Alteration of Type A Behavior and Its Effect on Cardiac Recurrences in Post-Myocardial Infarction Patients: Summary Results of the Recurrent Coronary Prevention Project." *American Heart Journal*, 1986, vol. 112, pp. 653–65.

page 156 "they are never a substitute": I have dealt at length with this issue of not neglecting medical care in favor of the paths described in this book, because I feel I owe it to you not to create false hopes—hopes of help from the paths I describe that, when they may not work to cure a serious disease, could turn to guilt. This guilt could arise out of a feeling that the worsening of the illness is our fault, the result of our not doing our best in applying the practices advised.

It is very important to remember that there are many pathways to disease, not all of them involving cynicism, anger, and aggression. Not everyone who develops heart disease or cancer (or who fails to triumph over it) does so because he or she had a hostile heart, or even any risk factors at all. Sure, there may have been something the heart attack victim could have done to avoid it, or to keep the disease from progressing after a heart attack. In the final analysis, however, this is never possible to know for certain in the individual case.

On average, we all do the best we can. Sooner or later, we will all die of something. There is never any real justification for blaming someone who develops a serious illness, or who does not recover, for not having done things to prevent the illness or ensure survival.

For it is never possible to be sure of what causes single persons to develop disease and die. The best we can do is try to reduce the levels of our risk factors so that we join a group with a lower average risk.

9. Let's Have More Trusting Children

page 159 "other characteristics besides *amae*": In case you are thinking I am proposing the wholesale adoption of all Japanese child-rearing practices, let me reassure you that I am not. For example, one aspect of Japanese personality that we may not wish to inculcate is the view of those outside our group (family, region, even nation) as not worthy of the same respect we show those who are members of our group. The use of shame—when the mother says, "I will accept you no matter what you do, but others will ridicule and make fun of you"—could be responsible for the aspects of Japanese personality that made it possible for them to be, despite the polite way they treat each other, very aggressive toward other nations at various times in their history, not to mention their current aggressive competitive business practices—practices many feel do not accord foreigners an equal footing with that of Japanese concerns.

page 162 "punishment—is much trickier": To illustrate how difficult it can be to be sure of how punishment, or negative reinforcement, is going to affect a child's behavior, I like to tell the story of the mother who visited the child psychiatrist, asking for help with her two sons, Jimmy and Tommy, who used too much profanity.

The psychiatrist, having listened to her tale of woe and concluding that the mother was "overreacting," told her to bring the boys in, whereupon they proceeded to curse in the most vile and profane way for about twenty minutes, without once repeating themselves.

The psychiatrist sent the boys out and told the mother, "Ordinarily I never do this, but, frankly, I've never heard anything like your sons—it's really even worse than you described. So, for the first time ever, I am going to advise you to punish them severely for this behavior. Don't do anything today, but tomorrow morning, the first one that utters a profanity, you must without any hesitation beat the living daylights out of him. That's the only way to stop this, I'm convinced!"

The next morning, little Jimmy comes down the stairs. His mother, standing at the bottom, says, "Well, Jimmy, what'll you have for breakfast?"

"Gimme some of them damn Wheaties," says Jimmy.

Without a word, his mother grabs him, hits him, stomps up and down on him, and tosses him out the front door, where he runs howling away from the house as fast as he can.

Calming herself, his mother turns to little Tommy, who has been watching all this from the head of the stairs. "And what will *you* have for breakfast?" she says to him.

"I don't know what I want, but you can bet your ass I ain't having none of them damn Wheaties!" he says.

Yes, punishment is really tricky.

10. Is Yours a Hostile Heart?

page 166 "Johnson displayed": Friedman, M., and Ulmer, D. *Treating Type A and Your Heart.* New York: Knopf, 1984.

page 167 "characteristic attitude": These often have the quality of "tapes" that you play over and over to yourself, often seeming to be on an endless loop, ready to start off whenever your cynicism string is pulled. It may help you to recognize your cynicism if you note the tapelike quality of some of your thoughts—they just seem to playing the same thing over and over again. If you get to the point where you can say to yourself, "Oops, here comes the cynicism tape again," you will be in good shape to start doing something to stop the tape machine in your brain.

11. The Behavior-Modification Path

The steps described in this chapter are based on a variety of sources, including my own experience in the use of biofeedback and other behavior-modification techniques to treat a wide variety of medical disorders (Williams, R. B., and Gentry, W. D., eds. *Behavioral Approaches to Medical Treatment.* Cambridge: Ballinger Press, 1977); the experience of Dr. Friedman and his coworkers in the Recurrent Coronary Prevention Project (Friedman, M.; Thoresen, C. E.; Gill, J. J.; et al. "Alteration of Type A Behavior and Reduction in Cardiac Recurrences in Post-Myocardial Infarction Patients." *American Heart Journal,* 1984, vol. 108, pp. 237–48); and the experiences of many colleagues at Duke and elsewhere that have been communicated to me informally over the years. There is evidence that each of these techniques, if properly applied, can be effective.

What is new here is the way I have organized them into a twelve-step self-help program specifically designed for a reader to put into action for him- or herself.

page 183. "volunteer activities are likely to help you feel good"; See Luks, A., "Helper's High." *Psychology Today,* October, 1988, pp. 39–42.

page 184 "Norman Cousins conquered": Cousins, N. *Anatomy of an Illness as Perceived by the Patient.* New York: Norton, 1979.

page 184 "Benson's pioneering book": Benson, H. *The Relaxation Response.* New York: William Morrow & Company, 1975.

page 186 "Benson's most recent book": Benson, H. *Your Maximum Mind.* New York: Times Books, 1987.

page 195 *"Practice forgiving"*: Fitzgibbons, R. P. "The Cognitive and Emotive Uses of Forgiveness in the Treatment of Anger." *Psychotherapy,* 1986, vol. 23, pp. 629–33.

12. The Religious and Medical Paths

page 200 "Huxley quotes William Law": Huxley, A. *The Perennial Philosophy*. New York: Harper & Brothers, 1945.

page 201 "Jerusalem's Hadassah University Hospital": Fried-lander, Y.; Kark, J. D.; and Stein, Y. "Religious Orthodoxy and Myocardial Infarction in Jerusalem—A Case Control Study." *International Journal of Cardiology*, 1986, vol. 10, pp. 33–41; Friedlander, Y.; Kark, J. D.; Stein, Y. "Religious Observance and Plasma Lipids and Lipoproteins among 17-Year-Old Jewish Residents of Jerusalem." *Preventive Medicine*, 1987, vol. 16, pp. 70–79.

page 201 "Evans County, Georgia": Graham, T.; Kaplan, B. H.; et al. "Frequency of Church Attendance and Blood Pressure Elevation." *Journal of Behavioral Medicine*, 1978, vol. 1, pp. 37–41.

page 201 "aspects of religious observance": Kaplan, B. H. Commencement Address, University of North Carolina, School of Public Health, Chapel Hill, N.C., May 1987.

page 203 "no difference in overall death rates": Rifkind, B. "Gem-fibrocil, Lipids, and Coronary Risk." *The New England Journal of Medicine*, 1987, vol. 317, pp. 1279–81.

page 204 "*ketoconazole* may prove useful": Sonino, N. "The Use of Ketoconazole as an Inhibitor of Steroid Production." *The New England Journal of Medicine*, 1987, vol. 317, pp. 812–18.

page 205 "Paffenbarger": Paffenbarger, R. S.; Hyde, R. T.; Wing, A. L.; and Hsieh, C-C. "Physical Activity, All-Cause Mortality, and Longevity of College Alumni." *The New England Journal of Medicine*, 1985, vol. 314, pp. 605–13.

page 205 "effects of aerobic fitness training": Blumenthal, J. A.; Emery, C. F.; Walsh, M. A.; Cox, D. R.; Kuhn, C. M.; Williams, R. B.; and Williams, R. S. "Exercise Training in Healthy Type A Middle-Aged Men: Effects on Behavioral and Cardiovascular Responses." *Psychosomatic Medicine*, 1988, in press.

INDEX